FAMOUS COURT TRIALS OF MONTAGUE COUNTY

★★★★★★

By

MARVIN F. LONDON

Reprinted by Permission
Originally Published by S.J.T. Printers; Saint Jo, Texas; 1992

Copyright ©2018
Montague County Historical Commission
www.MontagueCountyHistory.org

6th Printing
ISBN-10: 1983704164
ISBN-13: 978-1983704161
Published through CreateSpace.com

INTRODUCTION

Well over 100 years of time have intervened since the drama of settlement was enacted by the early settlers of Montague County. The memory of events, as related to us by our forefathers, all of whom have now passed on, are growing dim in our minds, never to return again. Realization of these facts have led to the compilation of the events presented in this work.

The work itself is not artistic. The writer is not a professional in the art of composition, as the reader will soon learn. Errors will no doubt glare at the reader from every page. Yet, the facts themselves are here recorded, where it is hoped they will remain.

This work has been compiled from old court records, county histories, old newspapers, and from the recollection of events as told to the writer by many of the Old Pioneers mentioned herein. This is not a complete report, and may even be inaccurate in some respects. However, it is presented for what it is worth.

It is not the purpose of this work to simply dig up the dead past. Nor is it intended to embarrass, or to focus public attention, on any of the descendants of the persons mentioned herein.

The events reported herein, whether good or bad, are a part of the history of Montague County. Our history should not be forgotten and lost to time. History deserves to be remembered.

We can take just pride in that which is good within us. And from a study of our past mistakes, and that which is bad within us, we can learn lessons and reap valuable profits for the future. There is much that is good, and much that is bad, in the events reported herein.

It should be remembered that when most of the events reported herein occurred, Montague County was a struggling young county. Law and order was new to this region, and was extremely difficult to establish.

This work is respectfully dedicated to the Old Pioneers, both men and women, who gave so much to establish our present day system of law and order, and who also gave us so much more of the good life we enjoy today, and whose memory and deeds I am happy to help perpetuate.

Marvin F. London
May 11, 1974

Printed by
S.J.T. PRINTERS,
Saint Jo, Texas
1st Printing 1976; 2nd Printing 1978;
3rd Printing 1981; 4th Printing 1983;
5th Printing 1992.

INDEX

The Brumley Family Murders	1
The Hanging of Charles Harris	5
The Hanging of Nancy Hill	21
The Taylor Murder Case	27
The Krebs-Preston Murder Cases	29
The Burning of the Courthouse	43
The Killing of Captain J.W. Kerr	49
The Killing of E.O. Driskill	57
The Killing of Homer Crook	67
The Brown Brothers Murder Case	71
The Hanging of the Brown Brothers	77
A Bank Robber is Killed	87
The Killing of Walker Hargroves	91
The Killing of Porter Brodie	97
The Killing of Walter (Pat) Smith	103
Conclusion	105
Permission for MCHC to Publish	107

In Memory

MARVIN FLYNT LONDON

State Judge of 97th District, (Archer, Clay and Montague Counties.)
Judge London passed away Feb. 18, 1980.
My Sincere Thanks for wanting his Book.

Mary Lou London

THE BRUMLEY FAMILY MURDERS

In the early 1860's, during the Civil War, one of the earliest mass killings of white settlers to be committed by other white settlers was committed in Montague County. This was the killing of John Brumley and his two sons.

John Brumley and his wife, Mary Brumley, lived one mile North of Montague, on Salt Creek, on John Brumley's 160-acre preemption survey. This is the place that Paul Veretto acquired some time in the early 1900's and lived on for a number of years. It is on the West side of the Montague to Nocona road. The Brumleys had a double log house which stood down in the valley near the creek. The houses were separated by a gallery or veranda.

The Brumleys had six sons. Two of their sons, Bill and Dan, lived at the Head of Elm (now Saint Jo) and operated a trading post. They sold supplies to early settlers, cattle drovers and wagon caravans. Another of their sons was named Luke. The names of the other three sons has not been learned. Some of their sons were in the Confederate Army. They also had a daughter, who lived with them at the time of the killings.

John Brumley and his sons had been engaged in a feud, and had previously had a bad falling out with a group of men who lived in the county. Their names were Doctor Armstrong, Jeff Davis, Joe Boilston, Jack Patton, Bill Musick and Dave Cooley.

John Brumley awakened early one morning, as was his custom, got up, lit his pipe and walked out on the gallery or veranda. Mary Brumley and the daughter heard Mr. Brumley get up, but did not themselves get up at the time, because they had a Negro couple who did the house work and helped with the field work. Mr. Brumley was an early riser, and always enjoyed a smoke while waiting for his breakfast.

Soon after Mr. Brumley had walked out onto the veranda, the Brumley women heard a gun shot. They thought the old man had seen a snake, or an animal of some kind, and had killed it, so they did not get up immediately. Soon after they did get up they found the old man lying in the yard dead, and his partially smoked pipe laying by his side.

A couple of days later, these men who had killed Mr. Brumley went to

Head of Elm to finish off the two Brumley boys who lived there. When the men were approaching the trading post, Bill and Dan saw them and took refuge in some trees behind their building. The men pursued them, and in the gun battle that followed succeeded in killing both of the Brumley boys.

J.H. Cox was Postmaster at Montague at the time of the killings. He had known the Brumley family for some time, and had always liked and been friendly with them. He had never had any trouble with the other men, or even any hard feelings, but had just been good friends with the Brumleys. He must have been openly expressing his sympathy for the Brumleys, for one day soon after the killings these men showed up at the post office. They were heavily armed, as most men were at the time and in those days. They dismounted and went into the post office. Mr. Cox said later that by their actions, he thought they had come to kill him. They talked to him for a few minutes, went outside and talked among themselves. They came back into the post office and talked to Mr. Cox again. Then they went back outside and again talked among themselves, then got on their horses and rode away. Apparently Mr. Cox had been able to satisfy the men that he had not been taking the Brumleys' side in their quarrel, but was only expressing his sympathy for the Brumleys, who had been his friends for some time.

Two of the Brumley boys who were in the Confederate Army came back to Montague soon after the killings, together with some other men who were in their company, to hunt down and kill the men who killed their father and brothers. They camped out in the woods in the Northwest corner of a 160-acre tract of land that joined the townsite. This is the land that was later owned by H.C. Masterson.

That night they tracked down, shot and killed Dave Cooley. His body was found the next morning. Cooley had been shot with a shot-gun loaded with buck shot. He was brought into town and laid out in a building on the South side of the square, where the Ulbig Café later stood. He was pretty badly shot up.

How many, if any, of the other men who killed their father and brothers were ever killed by the Brumley boys is not known.

No court trial ever resulted from any of these killings. The people at that time were engaged in a three front war. Most of the men were in the army or the rangers. They were fighting a civil war, an Indian war, and a war against cattle rustlers, thieves and renegades who had drifted into the county to plunder, steal and kill. Many of these renegades were Northern sympathizers, and were all too eager to cooperate with the Federal soldiers and the Indians. There did not seem to be the time, or civil authority enough, to set up courts. Everyone was well armed, and each man had to look out for himself and his own. Killings were a fairly common thing in those days.

Montague County was at that time attached to Cooke County for judicial purposes. Cooke County was in the 16th Judicial District, which included also Wise, Collin, Grayson, Denton, Tarrant, Johnson, Ellis, Parker and Dallas Counties. There was only one District Judge, and one District Attorney for this entire district. We did not even have a County Attorney. The District Judge and District Attorney spent two periods, of only one week each, in this county per year.

THE HANGING OF CHARLES HARRIS

This record discloses the trial, conviction and punishment for the rare crime of fratricide, instigated, so it appears, by the father of the assassin and his victim.

Charles Harris was hanged in Montague on August 29, 1879, for the murder of his brother, John Harris, on January 17, 1878. He is the only person ever to be legally hanged in Montague County. The Brown brothers were hanged in Denton County for murders committed in Montague County. And there have been other hangings in Montague County, in which the law was not invited to participate.

Charles Harris was born in Missouri in 1857. He lived with his family until his mother died. He came to Texas in 1871. On December 20, 1877 he was married to Miss Josie Simms about 15 miles from Pilot Point in Denton County. He was six feet in height, well proportioned, but not corpulent. He had blue eyes and light brown hair. Nothing in his physiological expression or general appearance stamped him as a murderer.

Between the hour of daylight and sunrise on the morning of January 17, 1878, Charles Harris killed his brother, John Harris, in the home in which they both lived with their father, Charles Harris, Sr., on Farmers Creek about 13 miles North by East from the Town of Montague, by shooting him with a shot-gun. Death came instantly.

On June 3, 1878, the June Term of the District Court, 10th Judicial District, composed of Denton, Cooke, and Montague Counties opened in Montague. It opened in the two story frame court house, which was later burned on March 31, 1884. The following officials were present: Judge J.A. Carroll, who lived in Denton County; M.D. Herbert, District Clerk; A.L. Matlock, County Attorney; Lee N. Perkins, Sheriff.

On June 4, 1878, the Grand Jury, which was composed of W.A. (Bud) Morris, who was its Foreman, W.R. Willingham, K.G. Heard, T.J. Williams, Jas. Davenport, John Orr, Jasper Fields, Jas. Cheek, Wm. Dixon, Jas. McDaniel, Dean McDonald and C.F. Wilson, returned an indictment for First Degree Murder against Charles Harris for the murder of his brother John.

The case was set for trial on June 11, 1878, but was continued until Monday, November 11, 1878. On October 28th 60 jurors' names were drawn as a Special Venire, and the Sheriff was directed to summon them to report on November 11. On November 11th only 35 of those summoned reported. The Judge then directed the Sheriff to go beyond the court house yards and summon 25 other persons to complete the Special Venire. Court then recessed until the following day. On November 14th a motion to quash and set aside the indictment was overruled and the case proceeded to trial.

M.B.V. Shockley, for the State, testified that he knew the Defendant, Charley Harris, and also John Harris, the Defendant's brother, who, on the morning of January 17, 1878, was killed in Montague County, Texas, at the residence of the deceased, the defendant, and their father. Shockley lived about two and a half miles distant, and saw the deceased about an hour and a half after the homicide. The wound which killed him appeared to have been made with a shotgun, all of the shot, except one, having entered the left side, near the heart, and lodged on the right side just underneath the skin. The wound was such as would inflict instant death. Shockley did not see the defendant the day of the killing; and when he next saw him, he (the defendant) was in jail at Denison, on a charge of stealing a horse of Mr. Reed, who lived in the neighborhood where the killing took place. Shockley knew Charles Harris, Sr., the father of the defendant and the deceased, and saw him at the scene of the homicide soon after it occurred. He remained in the neighborhood only a few days longer. It was ten or twelve days after the murder when Shockley saw the defendant in jail in Denison.

P.J. Tompkins, for the State, testified that he knew the defendant and the deceased, and gave the same description of the previous witness of the wound by which the latter came to his death. Attorney Matlock showed Tompkins a leaf from a blank book, with writing on it, and Tompkins recognized it as a paper found by himself and Dr. J.A. Gordon, in a path near the place where the killing was done. Tompkins did not know whose handwriting it was on the paper, and was not acquainted with defendant's handwriting.

A.L. Shoemaker, for the State, testified that he had often seen the defendant's writing, and was well acquainted with his handwriting. Being shown the paper identified by Tompkins, Shoemaker testified that the writing upon it was that of the defendant. The writing on the paper was then read in evidence, as follows:

> *"To the Officers of this God dam County:*
> *when you come up with us, bring all of Texas,*
> *or you won't get what you started for, but get*
> *a good whipping.*   *Charley Harris*
> *D & Company"*

L.N. Perkins, for the State, testified that he is Sheriff of Montague County, and had charge of the defendant ever since he was put in jail. Attorney Matlock showed to Sheriff Perkins two documents marked "Exhibits B and C," and asked if he had ever seen them before; to which inquiry Perkins replied that he had. At this juncture the jury were removed, at the instance of defense counsel, and the prosecution proceeded, before the Court, to lay the predicate for the introduction of the documents as evidence to the jury. Perkins then stated that while he and Thomas Harkins had the defendant in custody, and were at the blacksmith shop for the purpose of having him ironed, the defendant produced certain papers and handed them to Perkins, telling him that they contained his confession as to how John Harris was killed, and that he wanted to make the statement, and had written it out. Perkins then, and before he read the confession, told the defendant that any confession he made would be taken as evidence against him. Perkins did not force, persuade, or influence the defendant to make the confession. The first Perkins knew of it, the defendant handed it to him, and told him that he (the defendant) had written it, and that it was his statement about the matter. Mr. Harkins then told the defendant that any statement made by him in regard to the killing of John Harris would be used as evidence against him. And then the defendant told Perkins and Harkins that he would not have killed his brother if it had not been for his father. The papers were then read to the jury as evidence, as follows:

> *Charley Harris.*
> *"First, my father would come up to me and*
> *say that John was going to drive me off, and*
> *that he did not want me on the place; and he*
> *would say that John was afraid that I would*
> *steal some of his horses. And when I was picking*
> *cotton for Mr. Wells, he told me to quit*
> *and come home and help pick their cotton, so*
> *we could get off to Sherman, and he would tell*
> *me how to get John off in a way that nobody*
> *would suspicion; and my father said that if I*
> *didn't kill John, that John would me. And so,*

when we went to start to Sherman with the cotton, he gave me two dollars for me to get some arsenic; and so I did, and came back. Next morning he told me to put the poison in the milk, and the poison was put there; but John would not drink the milk, and then my father told me that I had better go off and stay a while, but be sure to come back; and I told my father that I had no money nor clothes, and he told me to get eight dollars and forty-five cents that Calvin Morrow owed me for picking cotton; But I had traded that off for a pair of boots to my brother John. And he said I could come back, and I could get plenty of clothes in the house there at home; and so I did as he told me. He told me to be sure to come back. So I went off to Denton County, and married, and came back in about four weeks. I got up to Mr. Henley's on Sunday night. Next day I went to Mr. John Sims's and stayed there till the 16th of the month, and came down to my father's house, and he was not at home; so I went over to Mr. Giles Gibson's and eat my dinner; and from there I went to Mr. Johnson's, and I tried to borrow a shot-gun, but before I got there, I saw my father starting from Mr. Anderson's and I caught up with him, and he told me that John was gone down to Mr. Hawkin's near Gainesville, after the rest of his clothes, and that I ought not to have brought them up. And he said John would be back that night, and that Hales; and for me to be careful, - that John might be up there at the house, But he was not, and so I got the gun. And father said for me to make out like I was going off, - an so I did, - but to come back that night and kill John while he was feeding his horses, and I came back but did not get a chance that night until next morning; and he said for me to come back the next night, and he would get me some money *and a horse to get off, until he sold all of his property, and then we would go leave the country. I came back the next night, but my father was not there at the place; and my father had told me not to take one of John's horses, for it would look like he was implicated in it, - that there was some horses in the country close by that I could get, and get off on; but he said for me to stay close to Gainesville, and come up to Mr. Hawkins's in about two weeks, and he would be there, and then we would go off.*

*No more at present,
Charley Harris."*

*"My father had often told me that John's intention was to drive me off and kill me, so as to get all of his property, and that John was going to get rid of us in some way; and I would ask my father why John had any cause for it, and he said that John had threatened to take all he had and leave. And before me and my brother never had but one fuss, and father was the cause of it. And my father often told me that he would sell the property afterwards, and we would go off. So my father told me to write in my day book the cause it was done, and drop it close to the house, so somebody could get the book, and be sure to not say anything about him, so he could get off. Constable Spence has got the book in Denison,
Charley Harris, Esq."*

H.N Richards, for the State, being shown a memorandum book, Recognized it as one which he got out of the post office at the Town of Montague. It was directed to the Sheriff of Montague County, and Richards was a Deputy Sheriff, and took the book out of the post office and delivered it to the County Attorney. It was post-marked Denison, Texas, February 5, 1878, and was sent to the Sheriff by one Spence, a Constable at Denison; but Richards did not know how Spence obtained possession of it.

A.L. Shoemaker, for the State, again testified to his knowledge of the defendant's handwriting; and being shown the entries on certain pages of the memorandum book, stated that they were in the handwriting of the defendant.

The State then proposed to read the entries to the jury; to which the defense objected, because there was no proof that the book had ever been in defendant's possession, or had ever been delivered by him to Spence or any one else, and because the State had not produced Spence as a witness to show from whom he had obtained the book. These objections were overruled, and the State introduced the entries, which were as follows:

> *"Publish this in the paper, gentlemen and ladies. I killed my brother, or tried, just because he talked the way he did, and I got a darling little wife to mourn after me when I am gone. But shed not a tear o'er your husband's early bier, when he is gone. For she is all the world to me; I love my darling Josie better than I do life, and I hope to meet her in heaven, if not in this world. I hope God will protect my wife and keep her from all harm. I hate to part from Josie, but it must be. Poetry by C.H.: I have a darling little wife, perhaps sisters three; likewise my aged father, he shed his tears for me. Farwell to all on earth, but hope to meet you in heaven.*
> *Charley Harris, Jr."*

> *"Josie, this is true: if John and I meet, one of us must die, for his talk about me is too hard for me to take. And, Josie, I am going off, but I will send some money to St. Jo, on the 4th Day of July, for you to come; and, Josie, you Must come. I will tell you where to come first, By letter, but I will back it to John Sims; and When you write to me, direct your letters to Franklin Pemberton. But I will write first, and Tell you where I am at. So, Josie, I will send You money at St. Jo. And bring all your things with you."*

R. Cook, for the State, testified that the defendant, after his arrest upon the charge of the murder of John Harris, was brought before him, who was a Justice of the Peace. Defendant waived examination, and Cook committed him to jail. While in arrest, but after being warned by witness that any statement he should make about the killing would be evidence against him, he (the defendant) freely and voluntarily stated to Cook that his father had put him up to kill his brother John; that his father, some time previous, gave him a dollar and a half to go either to St. Jo or Sherman and purchase some arsenic; then he bought the poison, took it home, and put it in the milk, but John did not drink it; that he went off and came back, and, by persuasion of his father, killed John with a shot-gun.

Several witnesses for the State testified to the movements of the defendant in the neighborhood for some days prior to the murder, and to his efforts to borrow a shot-gun. J. Johnson, one of those witnesses, testified that the defendant was at his house the evening before the killing, and tried to borrow a shot-gun, but did not get it. Defendant told Johnson that he wanted a shot-gun to kill John Harris with, - that if John did not put some clothes back where he got them, he would kill him before the sun set, or by the time it rose again. Mrs. Johnson also testified to the same effect. It was in proof that, within a few days after the murder, Charles Harris, Sr., the father of the defendant and deceased, sold his effects and left the country. The record does not disclose any distinct or adequate cause for the unnatural enmity of the defendant and his father towards the deceased.

The defense introduced John Evans, who testified that he lived within sight of the residence of the deceased and his father and brother. Between daylight and sunrise on the morning of the killing, Evans heard a report like that of a shot-gun, in the direction of the house occupied by them; and, looking in that direction, Evans saw someone running, half bent, about thirty or forty yards from the house, and heard the report of three pistol shots. Hearing old man Harris hallooing and taking on, Evans immediately went over there. He found John Harris lying in the house, dead, having been shot through with a shot-gun. All the balls appeared to have entered on the left side, near the heart, and to have lodged under the skin on the opposite side. Someone in the house had a pistol, which Evans knew was the pistol of John Harris. Three fresh loads had been shot out of it. Evans had seen the pistol there two or three days previous. Old man Harris was at the house when Evans got there.

The above was the only evidence adduced by the defense. For some time prior to his trial, Charles Harris had denied his first statements, those upon which his conviction was principally obtained. He said that he did not remember ever to have made them. And some of those who had been with him the most since his arrest were inclined to the opinion that when he made them he was in a state of partial insanity, during which he scarcely knew what he said. Others were of the opinion that the statements were made at the suggestion of his attorneys, who hoped by that means to secure his acquittal. In fairness, it should be pointed out that no one took the stand to testify to such partial insanity. Also, if his attorneys planned to prove him insane, because of the statements they supposedly had him make, why did they fail to plead insanity as a defense? Harris did not take the stand to testify in his own behalf.

On Friday, November 15, 1878, the jury, through its Foreman, D.F. Speer, returned its verdict into open court. The jury found Charles Harris guilty of First Degree Murder and assessed the death penalty. Upon that verdict, the Court entered the following judgment:

"It is, therefore, deemed by the Court that the verdict (guilty) of the jury be approved, and that Charles Harris be condemned to be hanged by the neck until dead.
It is further ordered by the Court that the defendant be remanded to the custody of the Sheriff of Montague County to be safely kept by him to await the further sentence of this Court and Defendant is ordered to pay all costs of this prosecution, for which let execution issue."

On November 18th, the defense filed a Motion For New Trial. This motion was overruled by the Court on November 19th. The defendant gave notice of appeal to the Court of Appeals of Texas. In June 1879 the Court of Appeals affirmed the case by its opinion recorded in Vol. 6, beginning on page 97, Court of Appeals Reports. On June 30, 1879, the Court sentenced Charles Harris as follows:

"On this day the defendant Charles Harris being brought before the Court in his proper person in custody of the Sheriff of Montague County, and having been asked by the Court whether he has anything to say why judgment should not be rendered and sentence pronounced against him in accordance with the judgment of this Court rendered at its last term convicting him of the offense of murder of the first degree, and the judgment of the Court of Appeals affirming the judgment of this Court, and the mandate of the said Court now being on file in this cause.

It is therefore, considered and decreed by the Court that the Defendant, Charles Harris, be remanded to the custody of the Sheriff of this County, to be by said Sheriff closely confined in the county jail of said County, and that said Charles Harris on the 29th day of August, A.D. 1879, after eleven o'clock A.M. and before sunset of said day, to be hung by the neck till he is dead, as prescribed by law, and that the Clerk of the Court issue a warrant directed to the Sheriff of this County, as prescribed by law, and commanding said Sheriff to execute this judgment and sentence in accordance with the law."

In January 1879, the newly elected county officials of Montague County were installed in their respective offices. The Court was now composed of Judge J.A. Carroll; R.E. Brown, District Clerk; A.L. Matlock, County Attorney; Levi Perryman, Sheriff; W.A. (Bud) Morris, Deputy Sheriff. W.A. Morris was Foreman of the Grand Jury that indicted Charles Harris.

Many citizens and Christian ministers visited with Charles Harris during the two weeks previous to his execution. Between the hours of 10 and 12 o'clock A.M. on the day of his execution, Mr. Turner and his wife, F.H. Jones, Miss Sloan, County Attorney A.L. Matlock, Miss Hyatt, District Clerk R.E. Brown, County Judge R.D. Rugeley and Rev. S. Crutchfield were permitted to enter the jail and spend a short time in singing. Harris was calm and resigned. After the singing they all shook hands with the doomed man and bade his farewell. Harris manifested feelings at the parting. Rev. Crutchfield expressed himself as being satisfied that Harris was prepared to die, and said the condemned man told him he would soon be in heaven with his mother.

Sheriff Levi Perryman, with a carefully chosen group of 40 armed guards were at the jail. The best of order prevailed, although the crowd of people was very large and constantly increasing.

The gallows was located some three-quarters of a mile Northeast from Montague, just under the hill East of the cemetery, in a small grassy opening between gently sloping timbered hills. Early in the morning people began arriving at the site to witness the execution.

At precisely 12 o'clock noon the Sheriff took the prisoner from the jail and had him placed in a wagon, in which he was then taken to the gallows. Arriving there, they found an immense crowd of people assembled to witness the execution.

Soon after reaching the scaffold the Sheriff and Harris ascended it, together with Rev. Crutchfield. Harris looked pale, but walked up the scaffold with a firm, even step. Deputy Sheriff W.A. Morris then read the sentence of the court, and the warrant commanding the Sheriff to carry out the execution. This being done, Rev. Crutchfield stated to the vast assemblage of people that Mr. Harris had requested him to sing, *"Shall We Know Each Other There,"* and that after the song Mr. Harris would address the people. The song being sung, Mr. Harris arose and said:

"Ladies and Gentlemen: I am here to pay the penalty of the law. I am sorry this crowd had to be called together to witness my execution. I do not believe they could be called around a better heart. I had a good mother, who taught me to be good, and I had no idea of coming to this. My aged father has been accused of being guilty of this crime. He is as innocent as the angels in heaven. He is an old man; I have heard lately that he is sick; he may already be gone; I hope I shall meet him in heaven. I hope to meet you all in heaven. I pray God that you will never be called again to witness such a scene as this. I am the first one ever executed in Montague County according to law, and I pray God there may never be another, and I pray God I may be the only one executed according to law in the whole world. I love everybody in the whole world. There is not a man in the whole world around whose memory there clusters one particle of hate. I hope my fate will be a warning to all young men of this County. I ascend upon the scaffold high that others may take warning of me. My time has come, I must go; I do not dread to go, though it seems hard. I have been, and am now a friend of Montague County. I love everyone in the whole county. I love the prisoners in the jail; and here is the Sheriff, as good an officer as there is in the whole world. I hope to meet him in heaven. I love you all. I hold no malice against anyone. I hope this may be a lesson to all. Remember, you all must die. I am young; in the prime of life. I hate to go this way, but I must. May God watch over you all. Think of the dying man's words. I hope you may all think I am prepared. I hope to meet you all in heaven in a better world than this."

At the close of Harris's speech Rev. Crutchfield said that the condemned man had requested him, and as many of the people who were willing, to sing the song, *"Sweet Bye and Bye."* Whereupon, several hundred united in the singing that beautiful Christian song, Harris singing with them. After the song Rev. Crutchfield knelt and made a solemn, feeling prayer, in which thousands of spectators knelt and joined.

After the prayer, a few of Harris's old acquaintances, who had known something about his parentage and childhood life, while weeping and sobbing, called to the Sheriff, saying, "Levi, may I ascend the scaffold and bid Charlie farewell?" The Sheriff answered that a few could do so, but there must be no disorderly conduct or confusion. These old gray headed and Christian men ascended the scaffold and bid Charlie farewell in a most affecting manner. While this was being done the order that prevailed showed how perfectly they were controlled by the principles of law and order.

A few moments were spent by those who were on the scaffold, including the Sheriff and his Deputies, in shaking hands and bidding each other farewell.

At 1:00 o'clock P.M. Harris took his place on the trap door. He seemed calm and self possessed. He looked neat, dressed in a suit of navy blue coat and pants and a white vest. He looked around at the vast throng of people and bade them farewell. When Deputy Sheriff R.A. (Bob) Nix placed the rope around his neck the knot was placed on the right side. Harris requested that it be shifted to the left side, which was done. The cap, with its veil, was placed on his head and over his face.

Some time before his execution Sheriff Perryman asked Harris to select some friend to cut the fall. But each time the Sheriff mentioned it, Harris would always reply by saying that he thought the Sheriff was his friend. But when standing on the fall, the feeling willing to show his respect for Sheriff Perryman's feelings, he requested Deputy Nix to cut the rope that held the fall. Nix, after being requested the second time, consented, and performed the duty reluctantly, because demanded by the law, but with something of mental reservation. At 1:20 the drop fell.

Following is the report of Drs F. Johnson, Wolverton, McDougal and Love, who were present to make such examination as would enable them to report to the Sheriff that life was extinct. As stated, the drop fell at 1:20; 1:24 pulsations distinct; 1:30 pulsation slight; 1:34 no pulsation at wrist; 1:36 heart ceased to beat; 1:40 Dr Johnson, and the other physicians present, pronounced Harris dead. Cut down 30 minutes after the drop fell.

Court records reflect that Charles Harris subpoenaed Henry Hawkins, Lucy Hawkins, David Simms, Josephine Harris and Charles Harris Sr., as witnesses to testify in his behalf. The records do not reflect that any of these witnesses appeared. The records do reflect that none of them took the stand to testify in his behalf. Charles Harris, Sr. sold his belongings and left the county within a few days after the killing of John Harris. As far as can be determined, he never returned to Montague County, nor was he ever heard from again. What a sad ending for a man's life! To cause one of his sons to kill the other, and then to know that the assassin son was himself hanged.

Although no one seemed to have remembered Charles Harris during his hour of trouble, he remembered others. For he requested in writing that Sheriff Perryman bury his body by the side of his brother John Harris on Farmer's Creek. His request was granted. He further requested that the newspaper publishing the details of his execution be sent to D.W. Colvert, Colvert's Station, Indian Territory; Franklin Pemberton, Fayette, Howard County, Missouri; Mrs. Lucy Hawkins, Gainesville, Cooke County, Texas; also that Mrs. Hawkins will please read the paper and forward it to her sister, who has always refused to write to him.

Editor Roark, of The Texas Northwest, covered the execution for his paper. It is from his paper that some of the details for this article were taken. Under dateline of August 30, 1879, he published an Extra, which was headlined: CHAR. HARRIS EXECUTED! 5000 PEOPLE PRESENT. His story went on to read in part as follows:

"We have deemed it best to issue an extra sheet containing an account of the execution of Chas. Harris for the murder of his brother John, on the 17th day of January, 1878, together with such written and oral statements concerning the matter as Mr. Harris has himself voluntarily made from time to time. While we deeply regret the existence of the cause that made the infliction of the death penalty upon Mr. Harris a necessity, we feel a pride in mentioning the admirable conduct and management of Mr. Perryman and his Deputies while passing through this trying ordeal. The affair, in all details, was most admirably arranged and conducted. While the dignity and authority of the law was duly honored and sustained, Mr. Harris had extended to him all the Christian sympathy and feeling compatible with his situation.

We were more than pleased to notice the good order and Christian decorum of the vast multitude present. It was truly wonderful to see how perfectly that vast ocean of human feeling and passion, whose swelling tides throbbed and surged in five thousand anxious aching bosoms, was controlled. We doubt whether so large and orderly a company of people could be assembled, under similar circumstances, in any other county in the State. That the Sheriff and his Deputies, who conducted the execution, and the multitude who witnessed it, were preeminently governed by the laws of the State and the principles of Christian civilization, was especially manifested when, just before Mr. Harris's execution, a few old acquaintances, who had known something about his parentage and childhood life, while weeping and sobbing, called to the Sheriff, saying: "Levi, may I ascend the scaffold and bid Charley farewell:" The Sheriff answered that a few could do so, but that there may be no disorderly conduct or confusion.

At an early hour in the morning the people began assembling. The expression on their faces, and their general appearance, furnished an interesting field of study for the philosopher and Christian moralist.

Thinking men could not well suppress the inquiry: What particular principal of Christian religion, as taught by Jesus Christ and contained in the New Testament, sanctions or demands the infliction of a death penalty? Was it the spirit of Christ, as revealed in the gospel of love, that brought together this vast concourse of people? Will the execution of Charley Harris develop and strengthen in the human heart the spirit and principles of the Christian religion? Or was it a spirit of idle curiosity, or, what is worse, the spirit of vindictive wrath and revenge, and will it not weaken in the human heart the power and rulership of the Christian religion? (At this point a portion of the newspaper is torn off and lost, so that the Editor's argument is partially lost.) *The narrative ends with the following words:*

We have not made these remarks nor asked these questions in a captious spirit, or with the design of influencing the people to operate the execution of the law. Our aim has been to elicit inquiry and thought upon the subject, and see if there cannot be some better method devised for the treatment of criminals than killing them. The subject is a broad one – one of vital importance. Its full discussion will involve the discussion of every essential principle of the Christian religion."

Pictured above is a drawing showing the hanging of Charley Harris in 1879. This was the only legal hanging in Montague County. Shown are a few of the hand-picked guards and a small portion of the five thousand people who witnessed the affair. [Artist conception of the hanging by ART LYNCH]

Sheriff Levi Perryman, who presided over the hanging.

Deputy Sheriff W.A. (Bud) Morris,
who read the death sentence.

THE HANGING OF NANCY HILL

Since this work is entitled, *"Famous Court Trials of Montague County,"* this report probably should not be included. This, because the hanging of Nancy Hill was not preceded by a court trial; no court of law sanctioned her hanging; and the authorities were not invited to participate in her hanging. Nevertheless, in August 1873, Nancy Hill was hanged in Montague County.

The hanging of Nancy Hill was long remembered, and long talked about by the early settlers of this county. She may well have been the first white person ever hanged in Montague County. In any event, she is the only woman known to ever have been hanged in this county.

Nancy Hill was a notorious horse thief in the 1860's and early 1870's. She operated along the frontier counties, where police protection was hard to come by for the settlers. Civilization was moving westward. Already counties like Denton, Cooke, Wise, Parker and Montague were being settled. She operated along this line of counties. She seemed to have headquartered in Springtown in Parker County. She was usually accompanied by two or three men, who constituted her gang.

She is known to have stopped occasionally at rural homes in Montague County in quest of food. She would always make her identity known. She was said not to have been unattractive. She was a woman of ordinary appearance and looks, of average height and weight. She always wore men's cowboy style clothing, and carried two six-shooters. She was friendly, pleasant and always very generous with her payment for food. After receiving the food, and before officers could be informed of her presence in the county, she would be miles away. She was in her early or middle 30's when she was hanged.

Mr. and Mrs. Sam Atchison, or Captain Sam Atchison, as he was called, because he had owned and commanded a steamboat, grandparents of Mrs. E.R. Mangum of Bowie, moved to Montague County in June 1872. They had three children, Maggie, Charles and George. They settled on the tract now owned by the Mangums, between the Henry and Tan Turner places, near the old Bowie Lake.

The lad, Charles Atchison, was dipping water from the creek one day when he was surprised by Nancy Hill. She came to the house with him, and was served a meal. She thanked Mrs. Atchison and said, "I couldn't harm such kind people." Charles said that at the creek she asked him if he had ever heard of Nancy Hill. He told her that he had. She asked him if he was afraid of Nancy Hill. He answered, "Naw." Whereupon, she lifted a skirt that she had tied around her waist to hide her pants and guns, and displayed, to use his words, "A hundred pistols on her belt."

On the day she was hanged, Nancy Hill was jumped by a group of men near Springtown, where she had been appropriating other people's horses to her own use and benefit. Whether her men escaped, or whether she was cut off from them, is not known. In either event, she was pursued by these men, who kept in hot pursuit, until they caught up with her on Denton Creek, between Montague and where the City of Bowie is now located. Having caught up with her, the men took the law in their own hands and meted out punishment by hanging.

Late the afternoon of the hanging, W.A. (Bud) Morris was out looking for his cows when he found the body hanging from the limb of a tree. Nancy Hill had paid the supreme price for her stealing activities.

[Editor's Note: An article in the Dallas Weekly Herald newspaper (Dallas, Texas) from Saturday, September 27, 1873, states: "A correspondent of the Gainesville Gazette says that Nancy Hill, the notorious female horse thief, and harlot ranger, was hung in Montague county on Denton Creek, recently."]

On December 12, 1873, the Police Court, which performed the duties now performed by the Commissioners Court, met in called session. The Police Court was composed of five Justices of the Peace, one of whom served as Chief Justice, a position comparable to the present day County Judge. The Court on that occasion was composed of James M. Grigsby, Precinct No. 1, who was Chief Justice; A.B.P. Mayfield, Precinct No. 2; William Fanning, Precinct No. 3, R.A. Green, Precinct No. 4; Chesley Marlett, Precinct No. 5; W.A. (Bud) Morris, District & County Clerk; W.T. Waybourn, Sheriff.

On that date the Court approved for payment a statement of Wm. H. Slack, Constable, Precinct No. 1, in the amount of $18.60 for his services in summoning a jury and witnesses in the Coroner's Inquest over the body of Nancy Hill. The inquest was presided over by Justice James M. Grigsby, sitting as a Coroner. The jury found that Nancy Hill died by hanging at the hands of a person or persons unknown. The names of the men who constituted the posse were never learned.

For years the writer has wondered why a woman, like Nancy Hill, would turn to a life of crime, culminating as hers did, by hanging at the hands of enraged vigilantes. To answer this question, the writer has spent years searching for the answer to other questions, which would help answer the main question, such as" Who was Nancy Hill? Where did she come from? What of her family? Did anything happen in her life that would have forced her, so to speak, into a life of crime? Was she led into a life of crime by a man she loved? To find the answer to these questions, old court records have been checked, county histories, old newspapers, old stories have been checked out, and numerous people have been interviewed. The facts, so far developed, are set out below.

During the Civil War, many people, in both the Union States and the Confederate States, were caught up in the war and suffered because they lived in an area that was fighting on the side that was contrary to their beliefs. Many people now believe that they suffered the most. Many people living in the South thought that secession was wrong, but once the war was declared they joined with the majority and tried to help win the war. Others tried to make their way to the North. The same thing was occurring in the North, and Southern Sympathizers were trying to make their way to the South. Others refused to help in the war effort, and refused to go to the North, preferring to remain here and suffer the hardships. In the harsh years of the war anger mounted against the "Yankee Sympathizers," and vigilante groups sought to drive them from the South or destroy them. Many people were murdered; their homes were burned; their crops burned; their livestock were stolen. These angers, and these crimes, did not end with the war. It was many years before hostilities died down to the point where a "Yankee Sympathizer" was tolerated in the South.

One family, who were said to have been Union Sympathizers, and who refused to aid in the war effort, and who refused to go North, was the Allen C. Hill family. Allen C. Hill lived with his wife, Dusky Hill, and his children, Jack Hill, Nancy (sometimes called Nance), Katherine, Martha, Adeline, Eliza, Belle and Allen, Jr., on a farm just out of Springtown, Parker County.

Allen C. Hill was killed in 1863, during one of the worst parts of the Civil War, over what was said to be prejudices against him as a "Yankee Sympathizer." He is said to have been killed by vigilantes.

Jack Hill, the elder of the only two sons, was killed in Montague County in January 1873. He is said to have been killed by a man named Aaron Bloomer, as a result of some difficulties between them. The records that would reflect, whether Aaron Bloomer was ever prosecuted or not were destroyed in the courthouse fire of March 31, 1884. If he was prosecuted, and if he was convicted, he did not appeal. There is no record of an appeal in Austin.

In January 1873, Chief Justice James M. Grigsby, sitting as a Coroner, conducted an inquest over the body of Jack Hill. He is the same Coroner who was to later, in August 1873, conduct an inquest over the body of Nancy Hill, Jack's sister. Both inquests lasted two days. On September 29, 1873, the Police Court voted to pay Justice Grigsby $6.00 for conducting the inquest over the body of Nancy Hill. It is interesting to note that the same order authorized the payment of $2.50 to James W. Morrow, for serving two days as a juror in the Jack Hill inquest. The same juror served in both inquests. The names of the other jurors have not been learned.

A few days after the death of Nancy (Nance) Hill, a mob took the two daughters, Katherine and Martha, who were next in age, respectively to Nancy, from their home to a place about three miles Southwest of Springtown and hanged them.

A few days after Katherine and Martha were hanged, not being satisfied with their vengeance, the mob returned to the Hill farm house and burned it. As the remaining members of the family fled from their burning home the mob pursued and overtook them. The mother, Dusky Hill, and daughters Adeline and Eliza were taken to a point near the present site of Agnes, Parker County, and were all shot and killed.

The two youngest children, Belle and Allen, Jr., who were about 12 and 11 years of age, respectively, were not killed. It is probable that the mob felt that these children were too small to have been a part of the family policy making, and too young to understand why the mob was angry with their family. In any event, these children were turned over to charitable people in Springtown, who took care of them until they were taken over by Sheriff Wes Hedrick of Parker County. What finally happened to these two children has not been learned.

After these terrible events, the God fearing, compassionate and charitable people of the Springtown Community were actually afraid to bury the bodies of the Hill women, whose bodies were left lying where they were hung and where they were shot. Finally, Al Thompson, a former Texas Ranger Captain, and Dock Maupin, a former Texas Ranger, who served under Captain Thompson, boldly challenged the vigilantes by taking the decaying bodies of the Hill women and burying them in dry goods boxes in the cemetery of Springtown.

It has not been learned where the bodies of Jack and Nancy Hill were buried. It is probable that their bodies were never claimed by the family, and that they were given pauper's funerals in the cemetery at Montague.

What a tragic ending for a family, for the father and mother, and six of their eight children, to have all been murdered? And so far as can be learned no prosecution ever grew out of the murder of any of them.

The question is still, what caused it all?

THE TAYLOR MURDER CASE

This is a report of one of those very rare cases of patricide. In about 1868 or 1869, in the Town of Montague, William B. (Bill) Taylor killed his father, William H. Taylor, by shooting him with a gun.

Mr. Taylor lived with his family in a house that stood on a place North of Montague, on the Montague to Nocona road, that was later owned by Paul Veretto. Whether Mr. Taylor's wife was living or not has not been determined. In any event, he was the father of seven children, four boys and three girls. How many of these children were living at home at the time of the killing has not been determined. Nor has the ages of the children, except that Bill was born about 1850 and A.K. Taylor was born in November 1859. The other two sons were George A. Taylor and R.H. Taylor. The three girls were Elizabeth Krebs, wife of Ben Krebs; Margaret Patrick, wife of Andrew Patrick; and Rhoda Ann Savage, whose husband's first name is not known.

Ben Krebs and wife, Elizabeth, lived with their children in a log house in Montague, that was located on the site where the wagon yard later stood. This is the wagon yard that was owned by J.L. Nored until up into the 1920's.

Mr. Taylor was a heavy drinker. He would often get drunk and go home and curse and abuse his family. He went home drunk one night and asked for his son Bill, saying that he was going to whip him. Bill was in an adjoining room and heard what his father said. He put a pistol in his pocket, slipped out of the back door, and went to Montague to the home of his brother-in-law, Ben Krebs. The old man followed him, went to Krebs' house and asked for Bill. Elizabeth Krebs, knowing her father's disposition, told him that Bill was not there. Mr. Taylor refused to believe his daughter, and pushed open the door. Bill was lying in the floor playing with the Krebs children. There being only one door in the house, Bill had no way to escape. When his father started to enter the room, Bill shot him down. As Bill ran out by his dying father, the old man said, "See what you have done?" Bill replied, "I can't help it. You made me do it."

Bill ran off into the woods and hid for a long time. He was finally captured by Federal soldiers, who were stationed at Fort Richardson in Jacksboro. He was placed in chains and carried to Jacksboro.

This killing occurred in the years following the Civil War. For some 10 years following the Civil War a conflict progressed between the civil and military arms of the State, each striving to retain a hold on the government. The Federal Government had troops stationed at Fort Richardson. They patrolled, and had responsibility of law enforcement, in Montague, Wise, Jack and other nearby counties. There was a Fort Belknap located in Young County. Its troops patrolled Young, Throckmorton, Coleman and other nearby counties. Few civilian officers were allowed to bear arms. The Texas Rangers were disbanded. Military law was the order of the day.

Bill Taylor was later returned to Montague and tried for the murder of his father. He was represented by Dick Burdough, an Attorney from Gainesville. He was acquitted.

Some time in the latter part of 1873 or in 1874, Elizabeth Krebs died. In the meantime, Rhoda Ann Savage had lost her husband. So, Ben Krebs married his first wife's sister, Rhoda Ann. Rhoda Ann had at least three children by Savage. During the trial of the Krebs-Preston murder cases, Mary Jane Savage testified that she was 15 years of age; Johnnie Savage testified that he was 14 years of age; Anne Savage's age was not given. This testimony was given in 1877. It is not known whether Rhoda Ann Krebs had any children by Ben Krebs.

Soon after Ben Krebs marriage to Rhoda Ann, he moved with his family to his 160 acre tract of land on Denton Creek, about seven miles south from the Town of Montague. His home was about one-half mile from the England home. It was in this England home that, on the night of August 26, 1876, A.K. Taylor, brother of bill Taylor, helped his brother-in-law, Ben Krebs, and James Preston, murder the England family in one of the most atrocious assassinations committed in that century. These murders resulted in five trials, covering a period of some four years, that became known as the Krebs-Preston murder trials.

G.W. Cox grew up with, and played with Bill Taylor when they were boys. It was G.W. Cox's father, J.H. Cox, who was called upon to make a casket for Mr. Taylor's burial.

Many of the facts necessary to properly write this report concerning the murder of Mr. Taylor, by his son, Bill Taylor, were forever lost to time by the burning of the court house on February 25, 1873.

KREBS-PRESTON MURDER CASES

About midnight on August 26, 1876, Ben Krebs, James Preston, and A.K. Taylor savagely, brutally and inhumanly murdered William England, his wife, Selina England, and her two children by a previous marriage, Isaiah D. Taylor and Susie Taylor, at the England home on Denton Creek about seven miles South of the Town of Montague. Krebs, Preston and Taylor thereby became the perpetrators of perhaps the most horrible assassination imputed to civilized men of that generation.

On October 30, 1876 the October Term of the District Court, 10th Judicial District, of Montague County began. Presiding were Judge J.A. Carroll; A.L. Matlock, County Attorney; M.D. Herbert, District Clerk; and Lee N. Perkins, Sheriff.

The Grand Jury was composed of John J. Willingham, Foreman; B.F. Hodges, Jas. A. Strong, Wm. Broaddus, J.G. Hardy, Wm. Dixon, L.C. McNatt, P.S. Hagy, J.M. Grayson, R. Cook, J.C. Bryant, and J.P. Woodson.

On October 31, 1876 the Grand Jury returned an indictment against Krebs, Preston and Taylor, who was a boy 16 years of age, for the murder of England, his wife and her two children. Each man was indicted for each of the murders.

Five trials and five appeals were to follow, lasting over a period of some four years. Two juries in Montague County, and three in Cooke County, in their retributive justice, consigned the two adult defendants to the gallows, and Taylor, the minor, to the penitentiary for life.

The testimony in each of these trials was substantially the same, and was in substance as follows:

Harvey Taylor, the only survivor of the England household, testified for the State, and gave the earliest account of the events of that fearful night. He stated that the family had set up somewhat late, talking about home affairs and Isaiah Taylor's approaching marriage. After prayers, the family prepared to go to bed. Harvey took his bed out on the porch, were it would be cooler to sleep than in the house, and, as he lay down, he noticed three men coming down the road from the direction of the Town of Montague. At first he took them to be three brothers of his, who had gone to live on their preemptions. Harvey observed that the smallest of the three men came in at the front gate, which was about ten feet from the porch. The other two were large men, about the size of Ben Krebs and James Preston, and were crouching down as though trying to conceal themselves.

The smallest man came on the porch where Harvey Taylor was lying, and, pointing a pistol at him, said "God damn you, get in the house." The moon was shining, and the man was in two or three feet of Harvey, who thought he resembled Bill Taylor, (no relation to the Taylor children of Mrs. England) a brother of A.K. Taylor, the defendant, and so much like him that they might be taken for twins. When ordered to get in the house, Harvey passed into the North room, and saw his brother, Isaiah Taylor, in the doorway between it and the South room. The man came in and presented his pistol at Isaiah, saying, "God damn you, I told you I would kill you, and now I intend to do it." He fired, and Harvey saw Isaiah fall. Harvey ran out the back door and heard another shot in the house, and then heard several shots, and men cursing and women screaming. After the screaming he heard more shots, and then heard no more noise of any kind.

Harvey ran off through the field to the residence of Mr. Williard, distant about a quarter of a mile, and told Mr. Williard what had happened; and about two o'clock Mr. Williard and his wife and Harvey Taylor went over to the England house. The Williards stopped at the front gate, Harvey went into the house and lighted a candle, and there found his step-father, William England, lying on his face, and dead, having been shot through the body and his throat cut; and found his sister Susie Taylor lying on the walk in front of the porch, having been shot dead. His brother Isaiah Taylor was not seen until after daylight, when he was found dead, about fifty yards from the house, on the road that leads from Kreb's house. The last time Harvey saw his mother and sister Susie alive was when he ran in the house, after being ordered to do so by the armed man; they were standing in the corner, barefooted, and preparing to go to bed.

E.T. Van Hooser, for the State, testified that he knew Mrs. Slina England, who was shot on the night of August 26, 1876, and died the next night. Mr. Musick came after Van Hooser, the night of the murders, and told him that Mrs. England was at his house, shot. Van Hooser went over to Musick's, and there found Mrs. England, very badly shot on the left side of the back. She was in her right mind, and said she was bound to die. Van Hooser asked her if she knew who shot her. She said, "Mr. Van Hooser, do I know you?" Van Hooser told her he supposed she did, and then she said, "I know that old Ben Krebs has killed me and my whole family." She said nothing to Van Hooser about who did the killing, until he asked her. She said she knew the man well, and told Van Hooser to go to Krebs' house and arrest him and all others there.

On going to William England's house, Van Hooser found him lying about half-way out of the West door of the North room; his head and part of his body being on the porch, and his feet and legs in the house. He was shot through the breast, and his throat was cut with a knife or some sharp instrument.

Susie Taylor was shot in the body, and lying dead on the walk between the porch and the gate. There was blood on the floor of the North room, near the East wall, and two streams of blood from there to where the old man lay in the door; and on each side of the door-facing were the prints of bloody fingers, scraping down each side of the door, as if the old man had tried to hold himself up while sinking down, thereby marking his last struggle on this earth. There was a large pool of blood where he lay, and several pools in the house.

When daylight came, Van Hooser saw the body of Isaiah Taylor lying in the road, about forty yards South of the house. He was shot through the body, and was dead. Ben Krebs lives about half a mile South of England's, and in sight.

Dr. J.E. Stinson, for the State, testified that about eleven or twelve o'clock on the night of August 26, 1876, a messenger came for him to go and see the England family, who, the messenger said, were all murdered, except Mrs. England, and she was at Mr. John Musick's, badly wounded. Hastening to Musick's, Dr. Stinson there found Mrs. Selina England. She was shot in the back, and the ball had passed out at her breast. She was mortally wounded, and perfectly conscious that she would die. Dr. Stinson talked with her and found her to be perfectly rational. She commenced to tell Dr. Stinson who had done the killing, when he said to her, "Mrs. England, you ought to be careful what you state about this matter; for anything you say, under the circumstances, will be taken as evidence, and you might hang an innocent person."

Mrs. England then proceeded to say: "I know that I must soon die, and I want to tell you all about it. Old Ben Krebs has killed me and my family. Last night we sat up late, talking about the approaching marriage of our son Isaiah Taylor. We had just finished prayers. My son Harvey had gone out on the porch to lie down. Soon afterwards he came rushing into the room, and a man behind him. The man shot my son Isaiah Taylor, and, as me and my daughter Susie ran out of the room, barefooted, old Ben Krebs followed us out. We scrambled over the yard fence and ran down towards the cow-lot gate, old Ben Krebs following us, shooting at us, and cursing us all the time. We were screaming, and Susie said, "Mother, old Ben Krebs is come to kill us all." Krebs said, "God damn you, you need not scream; I have come to kill you, and God damn you, I am going to do it." When we ran towards the cow-lot gate, he headed us off and got between us and the gate. We then turned and ran back towards the gate in front of the porch, on the West side of the house. Susie and I were together; she was clinging to me. Ben Krebs was shooting at us and cursing all the time. When he shot me I fell against the fence, and I did not see Susie any more, but in a moment I heard Susie cry out, "Oh, Mother, Krebs has killed me." I lay there for a few moments, and, after recovering a little, I heard my husband, William England, calling me. I rushed into the house with Krebs after me, and there I saw my husband sitting in a chair next to the East wall, with either James Preston or a Dutchman, who had stayed at our house the day before, pulling his head back by the hair and cutting his throat with a knife. I ran close enough by him to brush his knees with my dress. Krebs was still after me, and I ran out of the back door into the yard, and from there into the garden, where I fainted. After resting a little bit, I got up, and pulled up one of the garden pickets and went into the cotton field. I fainted several times before I got to Mr. Musick's. When I got there I told Mr. Musick who had killed me. He took me into the house and sent for the doctor.

Dr. Stinson, after relating the declarations of Mrs. England, stated that before day he and others went over to William England's house. His description of the scene of the slaughter was the same, in substance, as that previously given by Harvey Taylor and Van Hooser. Cross examination elicited nothing further, except that Mrs. England also said that when Krebs shot her she was close enough to him to have put her hands in his whiskers, and that on the next morning Dr. Stinson saw Krebs and Preston when they were arrested, and Krebs had on a clean shirt.

County Attorney A.L. Matlock, for the State, testified that on Sunday morning, August 27, 1876, he was informed that the England family had been murdered by somebody; and, being County Attorney, he mounted his horse and hurried to the scene. He reached there about nine o'clock, and found quite a number of persons already there. Entering the house, he found Mrs. Selina England in one of the back rooms, mortally wounded. He knelt down by her and whispered to her, and asked her to tell him who it was that had murdered her family. She was perfectly rational; knew Matlock, and all about what was passing, and told him she knew she was going to die. She said that Ben Krebs and either James Preston or a Dutchman, who had been at her house the evening before, were the two parties who had done the evil deeds. Matlock then went out and arrested Krebs, who was standing in the crowd, and also Preston, who was near by. Attorney Matlock and Sheriff Lee N. Perkins then arrested the Dutchman who had been at Mrs. England's the night before, and took him before Mrs. England, who immediately said he was not the man, and he was released.

Mrs. England then proceeded voluntarily to narrate to Attorney Matlock the events of the night before. His relation of her statements is substantially, and in many respects literally, the same as that which, according to the previous witness, Dr. Stinson, she gave to the latter during the preceding night, and, therefore, need not be here repeated.

County Attorney Matlock also gave substantially the same account as Harvey Taylor and Van Hooser of the position of the dead, and the indications of the savage incidents of the night previous.

Continuing with his testimony, Attorney Matlock said that he had Sheriff Perkins take Krebs into the presence of Mrs. England for the purpose of identification, and Matlock asked her if this is the man that shot her; and she said, "Yes" ... and Krebs said, "You must be mistaken; it must be your imagination." He said this two or three times. She then said to him, "Mr. Krebs, don't you feel mighty bad about killing my poor children and my poor husband?" He again denied it, and repeated that it was her imagination. She said, "I am not mistaken; I was close enough to you to put my hand in your whiskers, if I had wanted to. I knew you by your whiskers; I knew your face; I knew your Dutch talk; I knew your curses; and I even recognized that old white hat you now have in your hand." Krebs was then removed from her presence, though he seemed disposed to talk more.

County Attorney Matlock then preceded to search for tracks, and was shown one at the North end of the house, and said to be that of one of the murderers. On measuring it he concluded it was made by a number eight or nine shoe. He then, with five other persons whom he named, went to where Mrs. England had said that her daughter had scrambled over the yard fence. There Matlock and his companions found two small barefooted tracks, apparently those of a woman running, and going in the direction of the cow-lot gate, followed by a larger shoe track, which appeared as though made by a man. This track followed directly after the barefooted tracks until just before the latter reached the cow-lot gate, where it passed around and seemed to head off the barefooted tracks. All of the tracks then turned back towards the house, and crossed over into the yard, where, owing to the trampling of others, they could not be trailed. The man's shoe track was that of about a number eight or nine brogan shoe, with the left heel slightly run down; it was carefully measured, and was found to correspond with the track first found at the North end of the house. Going into the cow-lot Matlock and his companions found a track which they thought was the same brogan shoe track – the measurement being the same, and the track of the left shoe showing the same run-down appearance. Getting over the fence between the cow-lot and the cotton field, they found in the cotton field the tracks of three men. One of these correspond with the brogan shoe track already described; another appeared to be also that of brogan shoes of about the same number, with broad heels; while the third was a small track, with small heels, about number five or six, and appeared to be that of a boot track. These three tracks proceeded, nearly parallel with each other, towards the house of Ben Krebs.

Attorney Matlock and another of the trailing party followed the run-down shoe track until it crossed England's cotton field fence into the public road, and found it again on the other side of the road, where it took a dim path which led the trailers to Krebs' fence, which they crossed into his corn field, in which they followed the same track to a point within 150 yards of Krebs' house, where it was joined by the other two tracks, which others of the trailing party had followed. The tracks were measured at this point by the County Attorney, and were found to correspond exactly with the three tracks found in England's cotton field. They were followed on to within fifty yards of Krebs' house, where, on account of high grass and weeds, they could not be followed. The distance from Krebs' house to where the tracks were first found was called half a mile.

Attorney Matlock preserved the measurements he took of the tracks, and, on returning to Montague, went to the jail and measured the shoes of Krebs, Preston and A.K. Taylor. He found their shoes exactly corresponded with the measurements. Krebs' shoes were number eight or nine; the left one was slightly run down, while the right one was not. Preston's were brogans, number eight or nine. A.K. Taylor's were number five or six, with high heels, like boots. Afterwards Krebs and Preston were brought out of jail, and Matlock measured their tracks with the same measurements, and concluded they were two of the three he had followed to Krebs' house. All of the tracks followed through England's and Krebs' fields were freshly made, and not more than a day old. Attorney Matlock exhibited to the juries, as a part of his testimony, a diagram of the houses and enclosures of the England and Krebs, and showing the route of the tracks described by him. Matlock testified that the shoes of the prisoners were not fitted into the tracks. The prisoners had been carried off to jail before the search for the tracks was begun.

County Attorney Matlock further testified that a complaint and information for aggravated assault on William England was pending in the County Court against Ben Krebs, and England and his wife were the witnesses whose names were indorsed on the information. The cause was to have been tried on the first Monday of September 1876, about nine days after the murder of the England family.

C.G. McGuire, for the State, testified that, on the morning after the murders, he was at England's house, and was sitting on the wood pile as Krebs and Preston came from towards Krebs' house. As they came near Isaiah Taylor's body, where it lay in the road, they bore to the left of the road and went around the body about ten feet. They came up to where McGuire was sitting, and he observed that they were both very pale, and were trembling so much that he could see their clothes shake on them. Preston's pants were wet up to the pockets, and looked as if they had been dipped in water. McGuire was one of the party who examined and measured the tracks, and gave substantially the same testimony concerning them as that given by County Attorney A.L. Matlock.

Dr. J.E. Stinson further testified that on Monday morning after the murder of the England family during the previous Saturday night, he and three others went to search Krebs' house. Being assured that nothing should be injured, Mrs. Krebs made no objection to the search. Dr. Stinson asked for the shirt that Krebs had pulled off when he last changed clothes. Mrs. Krebs had a search made in the house and yard for some time, and at last little Mary Savage, a daughter of Mrs. Krebs by previous marriage, got the shirt down from the loft of the house, by climbing on the bed and feeling for it. It was tightly rolled up, and a shirt shown to Dr. Stinson during trial was recognized and identified by him as being the same shirt. He pointed out various stains upon it, and also a hole where he had cut out some of the stains, and had analyzed it and found it to be blood, though he could not say of what kind. After the shirt was found, Mrs. Krebs said that Krebs had changed shirts on Saturday morning before going to town with her – she having told him he must put on a clean shirt if he went with her. The family seemed surprised when they saw blood on the shirt. Arms being inquired for, she said there were none of any kind in the house except an old pistol that had neither handle nor mainspring, and this she produced, rusty and disused. After rigid search, the party found two pistols, other than the one she produced, one a navy six-shooter, with five fresh loads in it, and freshly capped, the sixth barrel showing that it had been recently discharged; the other pistol was a small cartridge pistol. When the six-shooter was found among some clothing in a little cupboard near the door, Mrs. Krebs expressed surprise, and said it was an old pistol some one had put there several months before, and that it had not been used for a long time. Upon further search, eight or nine moulded balls were found, of proper size to fit the pistol, and of the same size as two balls which Dr. Stinson had picked up in the room where old man England was killed. The pistol and all balls were introduced into evidence.

Harvey Taylor further testified that about a month before the murder of the England family, William England, Mrs. England and he were down at Krebs' corn field putting up the fence, so that it would keep England's livestock out of Krebs' field. While there they heard hogs squealing and dogs barking, and went to get the hogs away. A difficulty then occurred between William England and Ben Krebs. England pointing out to Krebs some cracks in the fence, Krebs getting angry and picked up a fence stake six feet long, and approached England in an angry manner and threatening manner, with the stake raised in striking distance of England. Mrs. England interposed, and told Krebs to talk to her; at which Krebs backed off and came again, several times, in a threatening manner, and said, "God damn you, if you come down here any more, I will kill you." Harvey Taylor said Krebs then took him down the creek and talked with him a long time, and said, "If William England is a Christian and does this way, I have no use for Christianity – hell is broiling for such men as he is." Harvey's brother, Isaiah Taylor, was not present during the difficulty.

W.Y. Nix, for the State, testified that two or three weeks before the murder of the England family, they, Ben Krebs and several others were at the blacksmith-shop in Montague. Krebs seemed to be mad; he had a stick, and was showing how a difficulty between himself and William England had occurred. Krebs said England had indicted him, and, before he would be sent to the penitentiary, he would kill the England family.

Jonathan Stroud, for the State, testified that, in July, 1876, he was traveling the road near Krebs' place, and met Isaiah Taylor and Bridgewater, and, while talking with them, Krebs and his wife came along. Isaiah and

Bridgewater went on a short distance, and Stroud had a little talk with Krebs about a thresher, when Krebs commenced talking about his difficulty with the England family, and, pointing a finger at Isaiah said, "If I ever get a chance at that damn rascal, I will clean him up." Krebs spoke about England's stock annoying him, and said he had been run over about as long as he intended to allow.

John Crier, for the State, testified that, a short time before the murder, he and James Preston, and others, were on a buffalo hunt; that Preston spoke angrily about the England family, and said they had been witnesses against his son; but Crier could not remember his words.

W.W. Richie, for the State, testified that, about sundown of August 26, 1876 (in the night of which day the murders were committed), he and his son were at Ben Krebs' house, and saw there together Ben Krebs, James Preston, and A.K. Taylor. A.K. Taylor had a shot-gun, and a little boy with him a pistol; they started off, and said they were going hunting.

Sheriff Lee N. Perkins, for the State, testified that he was with County Attorney Matlock when the latter went to the jail to measure the shoes of Krebs, Preston and A.K. Taylor. Sheriff Perkins then testified concerning the measurements of the shoes of the three men, and his testimony corroborated that of Matlock.

Mr. Rhoda Krebs, for the defense, testified that she was the wife of Ben Krebs and the sister of A.K. Taylor, and that she had known James Preston for about three years. She supposed that Mrs. Selina England was acquainted with James Preston, as he lived for about two years some two miles from her.

"On Saturday morning, before the killing," said Mrs. Krebs, "Ben Krebs and I were going to town. I asked him if he was going to town with a dirty shirt on, and I told him that, if he wanted to go to town with me, he must put on a clean shirt. I told him I would get the shirt for him. On Friday evening, before the killing, Ben Krebs cleaned two turkeys. He hung them up, tied by the necks to the upper part of the stable door. He then cut around their necks and skinned them down; then took out the entrails. The turkeys were hanging up about waist high; I do not know whether he got any blood on himself or not. On Monday morning, after the killing, Dr. Stinson and several other men came to my house and said they wanted to search the house for evidence of guilt. I do not know whether then asked for arms or not. There were two pistols, but I did not know it; I had forgot about the pistol being on the shelf. I had told Johnnie Savage (a son of Mrs. Krebs and a step-son of Ben Krebs) to put the pistol where it would not shoot any one; I did not see him put the pistol up.

"When Ben Krebs and I got back home from town, on Saturday, before the killing, James Preston was at our house. He was just going to start home. He lived on Sandy, about eighteen miles distant. This was about one hour by sun. I got supper, and we all eat, and sat around talking after supper. The wolves were howling, and Krebs said that was a sign the Indians would be in the country. We talked about the Indians awhile, and then went to bed; we all went to bed about an hour after dark. When we started to go in the house to bed, A.K. Taylor said he believed he would sleep out in the yard, where he could keep cooler. Krebs said, 'No, you must come in the house; you might take cold sleeping out doors.' I went in the house and made beds down on the floor. I and Mary Savage slept together in one bed, Preston and Krebs in another bed, and A.K. Taylor and the little boys in another bed. I and Mary went to bed first, and then the others came in and went to bed. We all went to sleep in a short time. We had been asleep two or three hours; in my sleep I heard some noise.

"Ben Krebs and I both woke up about the same time, and Ben said, 'What in the name of God does that mean?' Preston jumped up, and Ben said, 'Preston, don't go out; it might be Indians.' Preston and Krebs stepped out of the door and listened a few moments. Then Krebs came back, and he and I put on our clothes. Preston came in the house and put on his pants. When Preston and Krebs came in they appeared very much alarmed; and Preston wanted to know if it was Indians, robbers, or somebody drunk up at the pond, near old man England's. I heard guns in my sleep, and, after Krebs and Preston went out, I heard three guns fire. I tried to wake Mary Savage and Billy Savage up, but could not until it was all over. Ben Krebs, James Preston, A.K. Taylor, and myself all went out doors, to the West end of the house, and stayed there listening about half an hour. I was with them all the time they were out. The children were all in the house; there was no one else there with us. While we were out we thought we heard a woman screaming; but the dog was barking, at old man England's, and the wolves howling so that we could not tell what it was. We went back into the house and talked the matter over, and came to the conclusion that it was not a woman, but the dog barking, down at Mr. England's. They both said that, if anything was wrong, why didn't some one come and tell us about it. Preston said he believed that some one was killed. Tom Savage, my brother-in-law, came over the next morning, and told us that the England family were killed.

"There was a heavy dew that morning, and when Preston went out to get his mare he came back and his pants were wet up to his knees. He was always powerful wet when he would go after his mare and come back."

Mrs. Krebs testified further that she had seen A.K. Taylor put the gun upon the shelf near the door, where it was later found there by Dr. Stinson; that she told Taylor to be careful and lay it down so it would not fall and hurt somebody; that it belonged to her son, Johnnie Savage, and she saw Taylor, as he went out of the house, pick it up from where Johnnie had put it the evening before; that she had seen Johnnie load it on Friday before, and Taylor told her he had shot one load out of it at a turkey.

Mary Jane Savage, for the defense, testified that she was fifteen years old, and the daughter of Mrs. Krebs She gave a similar account to her mother of the movements of the household until they went to sleep; of Krebs cleaning and hanging up the turkeys the day before; of Preston getting his pants wet when he went to get his mare. Some time during the night her mother waked her and asked her if she had heard any shooting. She then sat up in bed, but she heard no guns.

Johnnie Savage, for the defense, gave the same explanation as his mother, of how Krebs was induced to put on a clean shirt the morning before the murders. He accompanied his mother and Krebs to town. When they got back home, James Preston was there; he had come there the previous Thursday night, hunting his hogs. He was waked up during the night by the firing of guns, towards England's place. Krebs and Preston were both at home; they jumped up and went to the door. He and A.K. Taylor went out doors with them; they stayed out doors for half or three-quarters of an hour. His mother was not out doors with them. The pistol found at the house by Dr. Stinson belonged to him; a few weeks before he had traded a hog to Jeff Hagler for it.

Anne Savage, for the defense, testified that, in a conversation with Mrs. England after she was wounded, Mrs. England told her that if James Preston was present at the time she was wounded and her husband and children killed, she (Mrs. England) did not know it.

Mrs. Fannie M. Van Hooser, for the defense, said she heard the dying declarations of Mrs. England, who said that Krebs killed her, and that if James Preston was there she (Mrs. England) did not know it.

S.J. Poland, for the defense, testified that he heard Mrs. England say that the man she saw cutting her husband's throat was just about the size of James Preston. Being asked whether Mrs. England said James Preston was there, Poland answered, "No."

Gus White and Louis Fisch, for the defense, testified that Krebs had on a clean shirt, going to Montague, on the day of the murders; they rode with him in the wagon, and noticed his shirt.

Andy Patrick, for the defense, said that on the same Saturday Krebs took dinner with him in Montague, and he noticed that Krebs had on a clean shirt.

W.H. Grigsby, for the defense, testified that he and his law partner, Frank Willis, had been employed by Krebs to defend him against a charge of aggravated assault on William England, and that he had informed Krebs that the highest punishment for that offense was a fine of not less than $100.00 nor more than $1,000.00, with confinement in the county jail not more than two years; that Krebs might also be convicted of only simple assault; that he (Grigsby) felt that he could beat the case.

D.D. White, for the State, testified that Krebs, when he came to Montague on Saturday, had on a dirty shirt; he described the shirt Krebs was wearing, and when shown the shirt obtained by Dr. Stinson, at the Krebs house, and introduced in evidence, said that to the best of his belief it was the shirt that Krebs was wearing in Montague on Saturday, August 26, 1876.

Thus concludes the testimony of perhaps the most brutal murders ever recorded in the annals of criminal jurisprudence of our county, and ever written in blood across the pages of Montague County history.

Ben Krebs went to trial in Montague County on November 10, 1876. On November 11, 1876, the jury returned a verdict of guilty of murder, first degree, and assessed the death penalty. Cash McDonald was foreman of the jury. He appealed and the case was reversed.

Krebs was next tried in Cooke County, on a change of venue, with Judge J.A. Carroll presiding, and County Attorney A.L. Matlock prosecuting, in February 1879. The jury returned a verdict of guilty of murder, first degree, and assessed the death penalty. Krebs again appealed. The case was affirmed.

Krebs was represented by Attorneys W.J. Sparks; Grigsby and Willis;

and N.P. Jackson.

Krebs' death sentence was commuted to a life sentence in the penitentiary. He served twenty-five years and was paroled by Gov. Hogg.

James Preston was tried in Cooke County, on a change of venue, on July 9, 1877. He was found guilty of murder, first degree, by the jury, and the death penalty assessed. He appealed and the case was reversed.

Preston was next tried in Cooke County in 1880. He was again found guilty of murder, first degree, by the jury, and the death penalty was again assessed. He again appealed. The case was affirmed.

Preston's death sentence was commuted to life sentence in the penitentiary. He served twenty-five years and was paroled by Gov. Hogg.

Preston was represented by Attorneys W.J. Sparks; Grigsby and Willis; Hurt and Williams; Crawford and Smith.

A.K. Taylor was tried in Montague County on June 11, 1877. On June 12th, the jury returned its verdict of guilty of murder, first degree, and assessed his punishment at life in the penitentiary. He appealed. The case was affirmed. L. Banister was foreman of the jury.

Taylor was represented by Attorneys Grigsby and Willis.

A.K. Taylor served twenty years and was paroled.

[Editor's Note:

This page of the original book by Marvin London showed a photo of what was thought at the time to be the 1884 courthouse fire. It has since been determined that the photo was not of this event, and therefore it has not been reprinted on this page of this book's reprinting].

THE BURNING OF THE COURTHOUSE

In the early morning hours of March 31, 1884, the courthouse in Montague was burned by three men. They were William M. Clark and Frank Clark, brothers, and Landy Howell. This was the two story frame courthouse, with rock basement, which had been constructed in 1873. It was located in the center of the public square, where the present courthouse now stands. *[Editor's Note: it has since been determined that the courthouse fire of 1884 was of a stone building constructed in 1876, not of the two-story frame courthouse which was burned in 1873].*

The fire was discovered by local citizens about 1:00 o'clock in the morning. Those who penetrated the burning building before its demolition discovered that the floors and walls at points where the fire was raging, and where the furniture in the court room, and in some of the office apartments, had been thoroughly saturated with coal oil, and that the odor of that liquid pervaded the entire building. On the morning after the fire, some battered and disfigured coal oil cans were discovered in the debris. These cans compared with the filled coal oil cans of two merchants of the town, who, for prudential reasons, had long kept their coal oil supply stored on the sidewalk, outside of their stores, were found to correspond exactly. The merchants themselves deposed that they each missed cans from their coal oil supply on the morning after the fire.

No effort was made to apprehend the perpetrators of the crime, until after the building was so far consumed as to remove all danger of involving contiguous property, when the Constable of the precinct, J.P. Kern, summoned a posse, including John R. Clark, another of the Clark brothers, to examine the surrounding country for indications of persons either having come to or gone from the Town of Montague.

This expedition, however, was postponed until the next morning by a severe rainfall, the posse summoned disbursing to meet at dawn. The parties, except John Clark, met according to agreement, and, upon the eve of starting, met John Clark coming into town, horseback, from a North direction, who reported that he had been on Salt Creek, without making any discovery.

The party followed John Clark's horse tracks, going and coming, to the place where William M. Clark lived, about four miles distant, having en route been joined by Sheriff L.L. McLain. John Clark's horse tracks, both ways, had been made since the rain. No one was found at William Clark's home, but several horse tracks were followed by the party to Floyd Jessee's house, where the party separated, two returning to town, and two, the Sheriff being one, going on as far as Ben Peveler's house on Cottonwood Creek where they found Wm. Clark, Bain Catlett and Ben Peveler putting up a fence. After the exchange of a few words, Sheriff McLain asked about the news. William Clark replied that he had none and asked the news in town and the Sheriff replied that he had very bad news, and Clark asked if anyone had been killed. The Sheriff replied that his news was worse than the killing of a man, that the courthouse had been burned. Clark, manifesting some surprise, expressed the opinion that the courthouse was fired by some party or parties under indictment, and said something about one Walker George. He said also that, being sick, he was up, off and on during the night, but saw no light towards town.

It was proved during the trial that there were one or more indictments pending in the District Court of Montague County against William M. Clark and Floyd Jessee for felonious theft, but that they had been pending through several terms of court, and that Clark had always been present when his cases were called and continued, and had never expressed or manifested any disinclination to meet them. By other witnesses it was proved that, on more than one occasion recently before the fire, William Clark had avowed his purpose to burn the courthouse, and by that means get rid of the indictments against him, and that he had sought the aid of Floyd Jessee, Frank Clark and Landy Howell in doing so.

Bain Catlett, who lived with William Clark, testified that William Clark, Frank Clark and Landy Howell went from William M. Clark's house to church early on the night of the fire. Catlett went to bed a short time after the parties named started to church, and waked up when they returned, and heard William Clark say, in reply to a question, and after looking at his watch, that it was twenty-five minutes past nine o'clock. Catlett went to sleep again without getting up. Some time during the night a man whom Catlett did not see, but recognized as John Clark by his voice, came to William Clark's house, called William Clark, Frank Clark and Landy Howell out to the fence, talked with them awhile, and rode off. Next morning, before he left his house going to Peveler's, William Clark asked Catlett if he knew when John Clark was at the house. Catlett replying that he did, Clark requested him not to mention the circumstances, and then told him that the courthouse had been burned. Before leaving home to go to Peveler's place William Clark removed the shoes from his horse, and requested that Catlett say nothing about it. He also requested Catlett, if the question was asked him, to say that the moon was about an hour high when he got home from church on that night.

Sheriff McLain told William Clark, Landy Howell and Ben Peveler, at Peveler's place, that the courthouse had been burned. When Clark and Catlett returned that evening from Peveler's place, Clark, before he unsaddled his horse, went into the house, got the overcoat which he wore to church on the night before, brought it to the door and smelt it. Catlett stated, also, that some time prior to the burning, William Clark, at his home, had said that the courthouse would be burned within two weeks; that the job was easily done by entering the North door, going up stairs, piling the furniture together, and applying coal oil and a lighted match, and that escape through a window by means of a rope was easy. Catlett said that some one, Landy Howell, he thought, said one night some time after the fire, when they were all in William Clark's home, that all present were in danger of speedy arrest for burning the courthouse. Catlett replied that, as he had nothing to do with it, he was not afraid of arrest. Frank Clark then remarked that Landy Howell was talking too much.

Landy Howell, who, upon County Attorney J.M. Chambers' agreement to dismiss the case against him, had turned State's evidence, was the most important witness for the prosecution. He testified that, frequently before the courthouse was burned, William Clark had asked his aid to fire it. He went to church with William and Frank Clark on the night in question. When they had nearly reached William Clark's home on their return, William proposed to go to Montague and fire the courthouse that night. Howell replied that he did not like the idea, but that, if nothing else would do, he would go along and help. William and Frank Clark and Howell then diverged North, went through a pasture to some brush about three hundred yards distant from the courthouse, where they dismounted.

Howell remained in the brush in charge of the horses. William and Frank left, going in the direction of the courthouse. They returned within ten or fifteen minutes, and reported that they had secured coal oil from the sidewalk in front of two stores. They then left Howell again, returned in about thirty minutes and reported that they had fired the court house. The three men then mounted their horses and left. When they reached the road about one hundred and fifty yards from the brush, Howell saw fire issuing from the windows of the courthouse on the Northeast corner, both below and above the stairs, and from the North hall door. The cupola fell in after the party got off about two miles. En route home, William Clark told Howell to ask him, on arrival at home, what time of night it was. Howell did so, and William replied that it was twenty-five minutes past 9:00 o'clock. The rain began to fall a few minutes after the party reached William's home. The next morning, William Clark pulled the shoes off his horse, and he and Catlett went to Peveler's. Frank started to Montague, and Howell went to Floyd Jessee's with a horse he had borrowed the day before.

Ben Peveler positively located William Clark at home, four miles distant from Montague, at half-past 12:00 o'clock. He saw William at that hour at home, and obtained some castor oil from him to administer to a sick child.

Several witnesses who left the church with William and Frank Clark and Landy Howell, located them near, and going towards William's home, between 9 and 10 o'clock on the night of the fire.

The State introduced evidence, being records of the District Court, showing that Ben Peveler and John R. Clark then stood indicted for breaking open the jail of Montague County in the fall of 1884. Sheriff L.L. McLain testified that he arrested William M. Clark and Frank Clark in October of 1884, and had placed them in jail. This testimony would have had them in jail at the time Peveler and John Clark, broke open the jail.

On March 23, 1885 the March Term of Court began. Presiding were F.E. Piner, District Judge; J.M. Chambers, County Attorney; L.L. McLain, Sheriff; and D.C. Hart, District Clerk.

On March 24, 1885 indictments were returned against William M. Clark and Frank Clark for Arson. The Grand Jury was composed of W.A. Davis, Foreman; John W. Crain, Taylor Puryear, B.L. Mitchell, James Wylie, F.H. Jones, Clark McDonald, Nelson Keck, Peter Coe, David Jordan, W.S. Thurston and W.A. White.

On April 14, 1885, William M. Clark was tried before a jury, and was found guilty and a 10 years term in the penitentiary assessed as his punishment. He appealed and his case was reversed and remanded for a new trial. J.D. French was Foreman of the Jury.

On October 5, 1885, during the October Term, new indictments for Arson were returned against both William M. Clark and Frank Clark. An indictment was returned also against Landy Howell. The Grand Jury was composed of W.D. Allen, Foreman; G.W. Williams, Isaac Wainscott, R.A. McGrady, J.P. Stone, E.W. Giles, G.W. Campbell, J.M. Strong, Hiram

Wainscott, Bascomb Aikin, C.L. Ray and Henry Crouch.

On October 12, 1885 the old indictments were dismissed against both of the Clark brothers.

On October 26, 1885 the case against William M. Clark was transferred to Cooke County on a change of venue. The case was set for trial on November 23, 1885.

The District Clerk of Cooke County states that she is unable to locate the file concerning that trial. They have either been misplaced or misfiled.

The case against Landy Howell was dismissed on July 30, 1890.

The writer has always understood that both William and Frank Clark were tried in Cooke County, that each was found guilty, and that each was sentenced to ten years in the penitentiary, which was the maximum punishment for arson.

THE KILLING OF CAPTAIN J.W. KERR

Captain J.W. Kerr was a former Confederate Army officer, who was an attorney, and lived and practiced law in Bowie. He was 47 years of age; weighed about 170 or 180 pounds; was a stout, robust, heavily built man. He had been shot in the left arm during the Civil War. The left elbow bone had been removed. He had very little use of his left arm. His wife's name was Vesta. Late on the afternoon of July 2, 1885, Captain Kerr was killed at the intersection of Mason and Tarrant Streets as a result of a shoot-out with Tom and Sid Irvine.

T.E. (Tom) Irvine was 23 years of age; weighed about 170 to 180 pounds; was average height. He had been accidentally shot in his left shoulder at an earlier time. He had very little use of his left arm.

J.S. (Sid) Irvine was a younger brother of Tom. Tom was a lot heavier man than Sid. Sid was about six feet tall and weighed 140 pounds.

Tom Irvine owned and operated the T.E. Irvine & Co. Furniture on Mason Street, although Sid may have owned an interest in it. In any event, Sid worked for Tom in the furniture store.

Tom was described by some as being a wild and rowdy fellow, who drank quite a lot. Sid was described as being a quiet, even tempered fellow, who had not been known to take a dozen drinks since he had lived in Bowie.

Some seven or eight days before the day of the homicide, Tom and Kerr met on the sidewalk in front of Dr. Riley's Drug Store. Some words passed between them about a claim that Kerr held against the Irvines. Presently Kerr went into the drug store, Tom followed, and said to Kerr, "Captain, you have monkeyed with my business." Kerr denied the charge, and called upon banker Easley to support him in his denial. Other words passed between Tom and Kerr, and finally Tom asked Kerr: "Do you think I am afraid of you?" Kerr replied: "If you jump on me, you will jump off very quick." Thereupon Tom Irvine, who had been drinking, struck Kerr with his fist, and fell, and Kerr drew his knife and advanced upon Tom, attempting to open the knife with his teeth. Dr. Riley and W.E.H. Jones then caught Kerr, and Tom got up and threw a vase at Captain Kerr, striking him on the head. From Kerr's head the vase glanced and broke against a showcase. Tom accused Kerr of writing off for a claim against him that was not due, in order to attach his property, and remarked that he did not pay claims until they were due. Kerr denied this charge.

On the day before the homicide, a portion of the broken vase was found suspended on the sidewalk wall of Riley's Drug Store, to which was attached a piece of paper of which was written: *"Presented to J.W. Kerr by T.E. Irvine. Please let this hang."* It was proved that the paper was written by Sid Irvine. On the day of the difficulty, Captain Kerr attached to the vase, below the said paper, another paper, on which was written: *"Whoever wrote this paper is an infamous puppy. Whoever reads the first, please read the last."*

A few hours before the difficulty Sid Kerr was standing by the hanging piece of vase, with it's attached notes, and was showing it to people. He was described as not being angry, but was making jokes and sarcastic remarks about the vase.

Tom and Sid Irvine were in J.O. Ward's saloon about an hour before the shooting. Tom was drinking, and called for a drink and took it while in the saloon. Sid was perfectly sober, and did not take a drink. While in the saloon, Tom said to Sid: "Sid, you must whip Kerr or I will whip you." Sid replied: "I cannot do that." Tom said: "Well, you must whip Kerr." Sid replied: "I don't know that I can do that." Then Sid advised Tom further: "You don't want any truck with Kerr." Tom then pulled out a pistol, which he was carrying under his coat, and had stuck down in his waistband. He then informed those present that his pistol contained a load branded "Kerr."

G.W. McNew testified that shortly before the homicide, he saw Tom and Sid Irvine, Dr. Riley and E.L. Jarrett, an attorney, as they were standing together in the street, in front of Jarrett's office, which is in the rear of Riley's Drug, and which was some 30 feet from the office of Captain Kerr. Tom swore that he would go into Kerr's office, which Dr. Riley prevented him from doing. Sid told Tom that he could see Kerr on the street, and that he must not go into his office. The parties then turned and walked towards Jarrett's office. McNew walked across the street to Kerr's office, where he found Kerr and Squire Stallings talking. McNew, himself, from Kerr's office heard Tom cursing. He doesn't know whether Kerr or Stallings heard it or not, but both were in as good a position as he to hear.

A few minutes later, about sundown, Kerr left his office. He stopped in front for a minute and spoke to T.H. Matthews. Kerr had a letter in his hand and told Mr. Matthews that he was going by the post office on his way home. Tom saw Kerr come out of his office and started out of Jarrett's office to meet him. Jarrett got up and put his hand on Tom's shoulder and told him that he must not go out to Kerr, to keep away from him. Tom then told Jarret to turn him loose or he would knock the water out of him, and placed his hand on the pistol. Tom then approached Kerr and Matthews, who were in the street, going towards the post office and Kerr's home. Tom told Kerr that he wanted to see him a minute. Kerr told Tom to go away, as he wanted no trouble. He cautioned Tom several times not to bother him. Kerr and Tom walked on down the street together, Kerr still Telling Tom that he should go away, and Tom still insisting that Kerr should explain something. Tom put his hand on Kerr's shoulder and told him to stop. Kerr kept walking. Tom then asked Matthews if he knew where Sid was, and Matthews answered that he did not. They crossed on over the street to the sidewalk in front of Riley's Drug. Tom asked Kerr if he wrote that note, Kerr told him that he did. Tom then said, "I am going to make Sid whip you, or I will do it myself." Kerr turned around and said, "Now, Tom, I warn you to leave me alone. I don't want any difficulty with you." Tom then called down the street for Sid. Matthews walked on down the street and left them.

Kerr then walked off to the front of Evan's saloon, and started across the street towards the post office. Tom started down the street, and he called out for Sid again.

When Kerr had reached the center of the street, about half way between Evan's saloon and the post office, Sid went out to meet him in a fast walk. Tom had also left the sidewalk and was walking out into the center of the street. Sid walked up to Kerr and handed him a piece of paper, and asked him if he wrote that. Kerr said that he did, and Sid struck him in the face. Kerr staggered back and drew a pistol. Tom then drew his pistol, and both fired, Tom firing first. Sid then ran at Kerr and hit him. Kerr then knocked Sid down with his pistol. And then Kerr and Tom fired at each other again. Sid had a gash on his head from the pistol lick, and blood was running down his face. Kerr began walking backwards and the Irvines were advancing on him. After Kerr had retreated for some distance, up to where the public well was located in the intersection of Mason and Tarrant Streets, Sid picked up a piece of plank and hit him over the head with it. Several shots had been exchanged between Kerr and Tom while Kerr was backing up.

The plank broke when Sid hit Kerr with it. Sid hit Kerr just as Kerr had turned and started to run, or so it appeared. Sid then ran up and grabbed Kerr. Kerr was staggering from the blow. Sid threw his arms around Kerr and grabbed his right arm and held it. A scuffle then ensued, Kerr trying to release himself, brought them nearly up to Ward's saloon. While Sid was thus holding Kerr, Tom ran up, put his arm around Sid, and shot Kerr. Kerr said, "Oh." Then just before the next shot was fired, Kerr said, "Tom, go away." Kerr began to sink down, and Sid laid him on the ground. Witnesses all agreed that from eight to twelve shots were fired in all. All but two agreed that Tom and Kerr were the only two who had guns. However, two thought Sid might have had a gun, but were not sure.

Captain Kerr was carried into Crawford's Store, and Dr. G.W. Hayes was summoned. Kerr was later taken to his home, where Dr. Hayes and Dr. Riley saw him again soon thereafter. After he was taken home, Kerr said that Tom Irvine shot him in the side, and the reason that he made no better defense of himself was that Sid had held him while Tom shot him. Dr. Riley told Kerr that his wounds were not fatal; that he would rally and pull through, as he had pulled through a worse scrape when his arm was shot. About two hours later, Kerr asked if either of the Irvine boys were hurt, and upon being informed that they were not, he said that he only regretted that he had failed to hurt them. Dr. Hayes told Mrs. Kerr privately that her husband's wounds were fatal, and that death would ensue speedily. Kerr, however, must have known himself that his wounds were fatal, for he told his wife: "Vesta, wire your mother that I have been fatally wounded, and that she should come at once." The shooting occurred about six o'clock that afternoon, and Captain J.W. Kerr died at ten o'clock that night.

Dr. Hayes testified that Kerr was struck by two balls. The first glanced across the abdomen and lodged in the thigh, inflicting only slight wounds. The flash from that shot set fire to his clothes. The mortal wound was in the right breast. The ball, entering about four inches below the nipple and three inches to the right of the center of the breast, passed through the body and lodged in the spinal column. That shot also powder burned the clothing and flesh.

T.H. Matthews testified that right after the shooting, he saw Tom Irvine running up the street. That he had not seen or heard of him since, down to the time of the trial on October 24, 1885.

On October 5, 1885, the indictments were returned against J.S. Irving and T.E. Irvine for the murder of J.W. Kerr. The Grand Jury was composed of W.D. Allen, Foreman; G.W. Williams, Isaac Wainscott, R.A. McGrady, J.P. Stone, E.W. Giles, G.W. Campbell, J.M. Strong, Hiram Wainscott, Bascomb Aikin, C.L. Ray and Henry Crouch.

On October 24, 1885, J.S. Irvine was tried before a jury. The jury found him guilty of Second Degree Murder and assessed his punishment at five years in the penitentiary. Thomas Begley, Foreman.

Witnesses for the State were J.T. Stallings, J.R. Frost, G.W. McNew, J.M. Crawford, M. Wheeler, T.H. Matthews, L.H Rosser, J.W. Linnen, John Stotts, Dr. W.G. Hayes.

Witnesses for the defense were B.E. Green, an attorney, who testified that he had resided in Montague County since 1876; that he had served one term as County Judge (1877-1878), one term as County Treasurer (1881-1882) and one term as County Attorney (1883-1884); that he was well acquainted with Sid Irvine; that he was a peaceable, quiet and law-abiding citizen. C.C. Johnson, an attorney, who testified that he was not a partner of Kerr, had no professional interest in the case, but knew Sid Irvine to be a peaceable and law-abiding citizen. Also, Clark Arnold, Wade Atkins, J.I.G. Cowan, William Rose, Mrs. L.P. Hoover, W.A. Phillips, D.H. Taylor, Dr. H. Riley, W.T. Penn, Robert Tieves, T.G. Worley, Luther Raines, C.F. Bowers, F.S. Williams, A.P. Stephens, E.B. Partridge, H.E. Puryear, J.D. Frazier, Jack Sanders, R.L. Thompson, J.O. Ward, W.M. Spear, George H. Davies and John Stotts.

Some of the defense witnesses testified that they thought it was Sid Irvine, not J.W. Kerr, who said immediately before the fatal shot was fired, "Tom, go away." Others thought that Sid said, "Get Back, Tom, don't shoot any more."

A couple of defense witnesses stated that Kerr was trying to shoot Sid at the time Tom killed him.

J.S. Irvine appealed his case, and the case was reversed and remanded for a new trial. On October 28, 1885, Sid was transferred to the Tarrant County jail for safekeeping.

On October 18, 1886, Sid's case was transferred to Wise County on a change of venue. He was tried in Wise County in the first part of 1888, and found guilty by a jury of manslaughter, and his punishment assessed at five years in the penitentiary.

Sid again appealed, and again his case was reversed and remanded for a new trial.

A fire in the County Courthouse at Decatur in 1896 destroyed all records prior to that date. The present records to not reflect whether he was ever tried again or not.

Tom Irvine was last seen running up the street immediately after he shot Captain Kerr. Testimony given at Sid's trial was to the effect that he had not been seen in Bowie since. The records at the Courthouse in Montague do not reflect whether he was ever arrested, or ever tried, or what disposition was made of his case.

On the next page appears a plat prepared by J.R. Frost, showing the main block of Mason Street as it appeared in 1885.

Statement of the case.

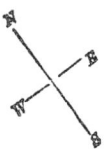

THE KILLING OF E.O. DRISKILL

On the morning of March 15, 1879, John W. McLaughlin shot and killed E.O. Driskill in the Town of Burlington, which is now named Spanish Fort.

On June 23, 1879 the June Term of court began, with Judge J.A. Carroll, County Attorney; B.E. Green, District Clerk; R.E. Brown, and Sheriff Levi Perryman presiding.

The Grand Jury was composed of W.C. Turner, Foreman; F.M. Kinsey, L. Banister, C.F. Wilson, A.G. Arnold, J.E. Willett, C.G. McGuire, Isaac Wainscott, J.A. Murrell, D.C. Jordan, W.J. Jackson, and L.C. McNatt. R.A. (Bob) Nix, Bailiff.

The Grand Jury returned an indictment against John W. McLaughlin of First Degree Murder for the killing of E.O. Driskill.

On January 2, 1880 McLaughlin was tried before a jury in Montague, with L.B.E. White as its Foreman, which resulted in a hung jury.

David Lenox testified for the State, that at one time McLaughlin had been in the employ of E.O. Driskill, the deceased, as a bar-tender, but the business relations of the two terminated several months before the killing; that at the time of the severance of the business relations between the parties, or shortly thereafter, hard feelings had developed between them, on account of some vulgar intrusion upon his property attributed by Driskill to McLaughlin, and with regard to the collection of a sum of money due Driskill by McLaughlin. At the time of the killing, Lenox was in the service of Driskill in the capacity of bartender. Driskill occupied as his business quarters, a house fronting South, the front room being occupied as a grocery store, and the rear room a saloon. A ten-pin alley, under the same management, ran the length of the two rooms on the East, with a front entrance on the South. On the night before the killing McLaughlin entered Driskill's business house with a double-barreled shotgun in his possession, holding his right hand at the hammer. He was angry and asked where that "damned red-headed son-of-a-bitch" was. He said that he wanted to "settle with him." Lenox told him that Driskill was not in, and asked him to leave. He entered the front door of the front or South room, looked into the rear or saloon room; then in the ten-pin alley, and then went off. When McLaughlin had gone, Lenox sent Driskill word at his boarding house not to return to the store that night, but at a rather late hour he did return, with a man named

Freeland accompanying him. Referring to antecedent occurrences, Lenox said that he had frequently known McLaughlin and Driskill to curse and abuse each other when they were drinking. At about eight or nine o'clock on the morning preceding the day of the homicide, Lenox saw McLaughlin and Driskill quarreling in the street between the saloon and the store of L.C. McNatt, which stood East of Driskill's place. He did not hear what was said, but could tell that they were quarreling by cursing and abusing each other. About an hour later on the same day, Lenox and Driskill were standing in the grocery store facing a drug store West, near which, on the sidewalk, McLaughlin was standing. Driskill patted his rear parts at McLaughlin, and Lenox a few minutes later heard them quarreling across the street. McLaughlin asked Driskill what he meant by patting his rear at him; this Driskill denied having done. McLaughlin denounced him as a liar, and the two quarreled, cursing each other until Peace Justice John Orr came on the scene and commanded the peace, and they desisted.

When the shooting occurred next day, Lenox was standing near the door leading from the grocery store into the saloon room. In going back from this door to the saloon counter, Lenox noticed the man Freeland near the billiard table, coming apparently from the West door of the saloon room and going in the direction of the front room. The shooting was then in progress. When the firing was over, Lenox, in going into the front from the saloon room, met Driskill at the door between the two rooms. He was staggering and reeling, and Lenox laid him on the billiard table in the saloon room, where, in about one-half hour, he died.

Lenox said that he and Driskill had often discussed the various difficulties in which he, Lenox, and Driskill had been engaged, and Driskill had often promised to "see him through" any in which he, Lenox, should become involved in the future, and had told him that he, Driskill, knew where there was a good place for a hog ranch in the Indian Nation; and that he would furnish Lenox and his brother, who lived in Red River County, some means, and would send Lenox his family from Weatherford, Texas. In none of these conversations did Driskill say to Lenox that he would aid him in the manner suggested if he, Lenox, would kill McLaughlin, though Driskill may have had such an idea in his mind at the time. Their conversations were of difficulties in general. Some five or six days before the killing, McLaughlin had a difficulty in the saloon with a man named Baxter, who had been about Burlington a short time. They both drew knives, and when, after McLaughlin had finally left, Baxter said that he was "very near killing" McLaughlin, and Driskill said to him, if he had it would not have cost him a cent. Baxter replied that he had money, and displayed a pocket book containing several hundred dollars. He said he was a son of the Governor of Arkansas, and he had left trouble behind; "was on the skip." At daylight one morning, two or three days before the killing, Lenox and Driskill were standing together in the saloon when some one came to the side door. Driskill placed himself against the wall to one side of the door, with his hand on his pistol, and told Lenox to open the door, that "this is as good a chance as I will ever get." Lenox declined to do as requested, thinking there would be a difficulty. He told the party to go to the front door, on opening which, he found it to be Jason White in quest of whiskey for a case of sickness.

On the night before the shooting, when Driskill and Freeland came to the saloon, after some talk about McLaughlin coming to the saloon with a shotgun, Freeland and Driskill looked at their pistols, and took a drink. Driskill asked Lenox if he, Lenox, wanted any stock in this matter. Lenox replied that he did not; to which Driskill responded: "You are a very good bar-tender, but no account in a fight. Freeland will do." Freeland said: "Yes, by God, I am Charley at the wheel; I am on the skip for trouble I left in Tennessee." When Driskill, after being shot, was placed on the billiard table, his pocket book was exposed and Freeland reached and took it, but on request of Lenox delivered it to him. It was found to contain $95.00. The killing occurred on Saturday, and Freeland left town on the following Monday, and had not been seen or heard of since. He left his shoemaker's tools in his shop. Lenox told him, Freeland, that he was accused of shooting at McLaughlin from the alley door, and advised him to leave.

About a week before the killing, McLaughlin, who was drunk, came into the saloon and got into a quarrel with Driskill; Driskill accusing him of having answered a call to nature in the ten-pin alley. McLaughlin said that he would do that wherever it should please him, even on the counter. Lenox had seen McLaughlin preparing to perform this operation in the alleyway some time before, but prevailed on him to desist.

L.C. McNatt testified, for the State, that at the time of the killing his dry goods store was situated on the Northeast corner of the square, in Burlington, and East of Driskill's business. At about sun-down, the evening before the shooting, Driskill came to the McNatt store for his mail, and while there was approached by McLaughlin with the demand: "By God, why did you put my account in the hands of an officer?" To which Driskill responded, "Because I could get no settlement out of you." McLaughlin replied that the amount was not correct, and that he had been charged with things he did not get. Driskill replied to this by saying that if McLaughlin said he had been charged with things not furnished him, he lied. McLaughlin said that either Driskill or some of his clerks had charged him with things he did not get. They continued to quarrel and abuse each other until finally McNatt told them to desist and go to supper. McNatt then went into his house, but, going out again every shortly, met McLaughlin going in the house, but did not see Driskill anywhere about. McNatt went to supper, and returning about dark, saw McLaughlin on the porch of his store, holding a shotgun down by his side. McNatt went into his store and did not know where McLaughlin went. From McNatt's porch to the usual pass-way of Driskill, to and from his supper, the distance is about thirty or forty yards.

McNatt was in his store next day, when the killing took place, and heard the first shot, after which the firing became rapid, about six to nine shots being fired. After the firing ceased, McLaughlin ran by McNatt's store, and left his pistol on a box in front. There were four barrels freshly discharged.

McNatt stated that he had paid or agreed to pay G.W. Barefoot $25.00 to assist in securing counsel to aid in the prosecution of McLaughlin, and had also signed, as security for the heirs of Driskill, a note for $300.00 for the same purpose. Barefoot was the partner of Driskill, and later Administrator of his estate.

The pistol used by McLaughlin in the killing belonged to one Howard Laforce.

Wade Horton testified, for the State, that he was in the employ of Driskill at the time of the killing. He gave substantially the same account of the quarrels in the street preceding the homicide, and of McLaughlin's coming to Driskill's place of business the night before the killing, armed with a shot-gun and hunting Driskill, as that given by Lenox, adding, with reference to this last, that when McLaughlin left the store that night, he, Horton, went to the door and saw that McLaughlin was joined in the street by two other parties, one of whom was McLaughlin's brother.

On the next morning, when the killing occurred, Horton was in the S.W. corner of the saloon room, near a window from which he could see all that passed in the grocery store. He saw Driskill standing in the front door, and McLaughlin out in the street in front, and heard them quarreling. Just as Horton observed them McLaughlin shot, and immediately Driskill shot. McLaughlin's first was the fatal shot, Horton observing the dust fly from the back of Driskill's coat as the ball passed out.

Horton said that, having called Driskill on business into the store, and away from the quarreling in the street near the drug store, he advised Driskill to have nothing to do with McLaughlin; and that persistent aggravation would result in trouble. Driskill replied that if trouble came he, Driskill, would not be in it, but had his man picked, $100.00 in pocket, and a good horse in the Indian Nation. Horton then recounted, as Lenox did, the circumstances of the exposure of Driskill's pocket book after his death, Freeland's taking it, and on demand returning it to Lenox, adding that Freeland left the country within very few days after the tragedy. He further testified that, on each occasion of the street quarrels of which he had testified, Freeland occupied positions at McLaughlin's back, but did not see that he had any arms about him. On the morning of the killing, McLaughlin passed the store several times going from McNatt's to Stone's stores; and when Driskill would see him, he would shake some chains that hung at the door, and call him "big bull." Driskill always carried an ivory handled six-shooter, 45 calibre, pistol. It was empty after the shooting, held six cartridge shells, and was warm.

Henderson Cook, for the State, testified that he was present in the saloon the night before the killing, an corroborated Lenox and Horton entirely as to McLaughlin's visit to the saloon, armed with a shot-gun, and making inquiries for Driskill, etc.

C.E. Noyes testified, for the State, after detailing several wordy difficulties between McLaughlin and Driskill, including those referred to by Lenox and Horton, that a short time later leaving McLaughlin in the drug store (at which time he also noticed Driskill standing in the saloon door), he saw McLaughlin standing near the saloon door, with his hand behind him, under his coat; heard him cock a pistol, saw him present the pistol and fire, saw Driskill return the fire immediately; after which he heard several shots. McLaughlin had on a heavy overcoat, and his pistol was under it.

J.H. Stone testified, for the State, that at the time of the shooting he occupied a position about 30 yards S.W. from the front of the grocery store, on horseback, in plain view of both parties. Driskill was standing in his front door. McLaughlin was standing outside, in front of, and near Driskill. His hat was laying on the ground, 6 or 8 feet S.W. from him. They were quarreling, cursing and taunting each other of fear. They stood thus about five minutes after Stone first saw them, when McLaughlin drew his pistol and dropped it at his side; Driskill at the same time drawing his far enough from his bosom to expose the handle. McLaughlin then put his pistol under his coat, keeping his hand on it. McLaughlin again drew his pistol from behind him, and brought it down in front of him with the muzzle directed towards the feet of Driskill. Driskill drew his pistol from his bosom until Stone could see nearly the whole of it, and stopped. McLaughlin then asked, "What do you mean?" Driskill replied: "By God, I mean business; whet do you mean?" McLaughlin raising his pistol, said, "If I must, I must," and fired, Driskill firing nearly at the same time. Stone did not want to say which fired first, it was so near together. He was certain, however, that McLaughlin drew and presented his pistol first, though the actions of the parties were nearly simultaneous.

Stone stated that in his opinion there were altogether some eight or nine shots fired during the fight, but he could not say positively how many. The first two he knew were fired by McLaughlin and Driskill. Two shots struck near Stone, which in his own opinion could not have been fired by either McLaughlin or Driskill. A shot fired by Driskill, who stood inside the door, at McLaughlin, who faced him from outside, would not have coursed to where these shots struck. Shots fired by McLaughlin from the front of the store would not have coursed to where these shots struck, since they were directed towards the front of the store and at Driskill. However, shots fired at McLaughlin from the alley, running along the West side of the store and saloon building, would have had range with the points where these two shots struck.

Jason White, for the defense, testified that very early one morning, two or three days before the killing, he went to the West side door of Driskill's saloon and tried to get in to purchase some whiskey for a sick child, but was refused admittance there, and directed to go to the front door. On being admitted there, he found Lenox and Driskill. Very early on the morning of the killing, he went to the grocery store of Driskill to purchase some potatoes; after purchasing which, he and Driskill stood for a while in the door. During this time McLaughlin passed by, going towards the drug store. Driskill hailed him, asking where his snot-gun was, and told him he had best go get it, and when he got it to use it. McLaughlin remarked to Driskill that he was not armed, and Driskill advised him to go get his arms, and to be sure to use them, adding that it was no more reprehensible to carry a shotgun during the day than at night.

Isaac Beasley, for the defense, testified that he saw a quarrel between McLaughlin and Driskill, about dark on the evening before the killing, near

McNatt's store, during which McLaughlin asked Driskill, "Why are you always abusing me when you know I am not armed?" to which Driskill replied: "God damn you, go and arm yourself. I will bet you will not do it. I will stay here and wait until you come back and see if you do." McLaughlin went off towards home, and Beasley left Driskill standing near McNatt's store, and did not know where he went afterwards.

Beasley said that the shotgun McLaughlin had on the night before the killing belonged to his, Beasley's, brother. He did not know who gave it to McLaughlin. Beasley at that time was living in the same house with McLaughlin.

Byron Hill testified for the defense that, at the time of the killing, he was clerking in Stone's drug store. He heard some of the quarreling in front of the saloon, and about that time heard Freeland give three or four blasts on his flute and saw him start in a rapid walk across the street from his shoe shop, go in the West door of the saloon, turn as though he were going into the front room of the saloon, and about this time the shooting began. Stone, Hill's employer, had a Winchester rifle, which he had been keeping in the store, but which he had carried home a few days before. Freeland desired Hill to keep the gun at the store; and said some "Damn son-of-a-bitch" was going to be killed, and he would have to "skip out." He also told Hill that he should have the gun in the store, so that if either Hill or himself should get into trouble the gun would be "handy," and the two of them could help each other; that if Hill were attacked he, Freeland, could kill the assailant from his shop window. He told Hill that he was on the "skip" from Tennessee on account of trouble. Freeland left the country a few days after the killing, leaving his shop, tools, flute and horse undisposed of, and Hill had heard nothing from him since. Stone's drug store is across the street from and nearly opposite the West door of Driskill's saloon, and Freeland's shoe shop adjoined the drug store on the North and fronted the same way.

When McLaughlin was placed under arrest, Hill among others was placed in charge of him as guard, and one night McLaughlin escaped from them, into the Indian Territory, from which he was brought back by Constable W.H. Bagwell.

J.P. Stone, proprietor of the drug store, testified for the defense that in the morning, about one hour before the killing, while McLaughlin was standing in the drug store door, Stone saw Driskill standing across the way in his own door, laughing, dancing, whistling, and patting his rear at

McLaughlin as though to tantalize him, and he knew from McLaughlin's appearance that this conduct angered him. Stone advised McLaughlin, however, to have no difficulty with Driskill, and received his promise that he would not. Just before the killing he saw McLaughlin leave the drug store and go in the direction of McNatt's store, and saw that he, McLaughlin, was about to pass in front of Driskill's saloon, some one rattled some chains and reached out and knocked off McLaughlin's hat. He did not see the person who did this. In a short time the shooting commenced.

Freeland had tried on several occasions to purchase a Winchester rifle from Stone, but Stone would not sell, because of the difficulties between McLaughlin and Driskill, and Stone believed that Freeland was "backing" Driskill. Freeland tried also to borrow or buy a horse from Stone, but this he also refused. Stone did agree to sell the gun to Dr. Burns, a partner of Driskill, but finding, before the sale was consummated, that he wanted to buy it for Freeland, refused. When Freeland left the country, he left on foot.

Stone stated that on that morning and before the shooting, McLaughlin told him at the drug store that he had been drinking and was sick, and Stone gave him not more than two drinks of whiskey. Stone advised McLaughlin to have no trouble with Driskill, and he said he would not go about the saloon, and that he would be satisfied if he could give Driskill "a good whipping." McLaughlin lived in Burlington, was in town every day, but was engaged in no business at the time of the killing.

George Cisco, a witness for the defense, testified that while he was standing at a point about 75 steps from the saloon, on the West side of the square, he saw McLaughlin start from the drug store in the direction of McNatt's store. As he passed in front of Driskill's store, Driskill was standing in the door. After having passed the door, McLaughlin turned with his right hand behind him, and walked up to Driskill. Driskill struck his hat off with his left hand. Each then struck the other with the left hand. For some time they stood and cursed each other, when McLaughlin drew his pistol and held it down at the side, and Driskill drew his up from his beast pocket, and presently they commenced firing, but Cisco did not know which one shot first. Cisco saw smoke boil out from the alley door, during the shooting, as though some one were shooting from there.

Calvin Baker, for the defense, testified that he witnessed the shooting from a point about 75 yards S.W. from the saloon. His testimony was substantially the same as that of George Cisco.

Rube Horton testified for the defense that, a little after dark on the evening before the killing, he was in McNatt's store, where pat McLaughlin, John W. McLaughlin's brother, was clerking. Some one told Pat that his brother had gone to the saloon with a shotgun, and Pat went to the saloon to get his brother to go home. And early the next morning Horton told Driskill that it would be best to "leave McLaughlin alone;" that if they kept on it would terminate in trouble. Driskill replied that the row had to come, and had as well come then as any time; that when McLaughlin reached town that morning, he was going to see him and ask where his gun was, and tell him to go and get it; that he would bet $20.00 that McLaughlin would not get it.

Dr. Salmon testified that he was called to see McLaughlin shortly after the shooting, and found he had been shot twice; once in the left side, the ball entering from the front and ranging backwards and downwards very near reaching the cavity of the abdomen; the other ball striking square between the shoulders, passing through the over-coat and under-coat at the seams, and lodging without entering the body, but raising a bump.

McLaughlin was tried again on June 26, 1880 and found guilty of Second Degree Murder. His punishment was assessed at five years in the penitentiary. He appealed, and his case was reversed and remanded for a new trial. T.C. Pembroke was Foreman of the Jury.

McLaughlin was again tried in December of 1880. He was again found guilty of Second Degree Murder, and his punishment was again assessed at confinement in the penitentiary for a period of five years. He again appealed, and his case was again reversed and remanded for a new trial.

Whether McLaughlin was ever tried again is not known. The records at the courthouse which would furnish that information appear to be missing.

McLaughlin was represented by Attorneys Grigsby & Willis and Davis & Garnett.

THE KILLING OF HOMER CROOK

Some time in the early part of 1884 Henry Peter shot and killed Homer Crook, in the mistaken belief that he was shooting his, Homer Crook's brother, Leck Crook. The date of the shooting is not available from the records. However, Henry Peter was indicted for the killing on June 4, 1884.

On June 2, 1884 the June Term of court opened with Judge Clay C. Potter, County Attorney B.E. Green, District Clerk R.E. Brown and Sheriff G.W. Campbell presiding

The Grand Jury was composed of W.D. Allen, Foreman; C. C. White, I.J.G. Cowan, R.J. Brown, Wm. Evans, N.C. Smith, L. Bannister, W.A. Fincher, W.Y. Nix, Griffin Ford, E.W. Roberson, and Wm. Maddox.

On April 8, 1887 the case was tried to a jury before Special Judge J.W. Patterson. By then the public officials had changed. F.E. Pinor was District Judge, S.P. Huff was County Attorney, D.C. Hart was District Clerk, and G.W. Campbell was Sheriff again after having been out of office during 1885 and 1886.

The jury found Henry Peter guilty of Manslaughter and assessed his punishment at confinement in the penitentiary for two years.

Granville Kindred was a jailer in the Denton County jail. A few days before the killing, Leck Crook was a prisoner in that jail; he overpowered Kindred, taking away from him the keys and releasing himself and other prisoners. The above facts were made known to Constable Henry Peter.

Constable Peter had information that Crook had fled to Wise County. Peter went to Wise County, where he obtained a Warrant of Arrest from a Justice of the Peace. Crook could not be found in Wise County, but Peter heard that he had gone to Montague County.

Constable Henry Peter, D.C. Fondren and another man went to Montague County to look for Crook. About ten or eleven o'clock on the night of the homicide they went to the home of the father of Leck Crook to search for the fugitive. The search was not in any manner impeded by any member of the family; in fact, the father gave voluntary information leading to the recovery of a horse, which was part of the object of the search. Failing to find Leck Crook the party went into camp about a half mile distant from the searched premises near a tank.

Peter and Fondren went back and stationed themselves sufficiently near the house to keep up a watch. Shortly thereafter, N.B. Crook, the father, sent one of his sons, Homer Crook, out to see if the horses were securely tied for the night. The father and another of his sons, William Crook, remained in the house. Following soon thereafter the report of a gun was heard, and upon going out N.B. and William Crook found Homer lying dead upon the ground, near where the horses were tied. N.B. Crook said the shot was fired just as he was calling his son Homer.

D.C. Fondren, the only eye witness to the homicide, testified that when they saw the deceased near the pen where the horses were tied, Henry Peter said: "Yonder he is now;" that Homer Crook stood there for a short time, and while there was facing he and Peter; that they were squatted down, but in full view of Homer Crook. "Then he started in the direction of where we were; and when he advanced towards us about fifty yards Peter told him to halt, but he did not stop, and came on towards us; and after he had advanced a few steps further we told him again to stop, or hold up. As we did so he stopped and drew his hands up to about his waist; then Peter fired and Homer fell." He did not hear anybody about the house call just before the shooting. Fondren further testified that he and Peter went off rapidly in the direction of the tank without stopping to look at the body.

It was in evidence that it was a bright moonlight night, and that Peter was well acquainted with both Homer and Leck Crook; that he was friendly and on visiting terms with the Crook family, they having cultivated land belonging to his father in Denton County in 1883, the year before the killing. Also that Homer Crook and Leck Crook were somewhat alike in general appearance, though not the same in height and weight.

The other man who accompanied Peter and Fondren on the search for Leck Crook met Peter and Fondren on their return to the tank after the shooting, and he stated that, in answer to a question from him as to what had happened, Peter said that, "he had shot some one he supposed was Leck Crook, but was afraid he was mistaken as to the man," and that Peter then proceeded to detail the circumstances of the shooting.

Henry Peter appealed his conviction. The Texas Court of Appeals held that since the Warrant of Arrest was issued by a Justice of the Peace in Wise County, Peter had no right to attempt to execute the warrant in Montague

County; that he should have taken the warrant to the Sheriff of Montague County, or other officer authorized to execute Warrants of Arrest in Montague County. The case was affirmed on June 24, 1887.

Peter was represented by Attorneys E.C. Smith and W.S. Jameson.

THE BROWN BROTHERS MURDER CASE

On November 1, 1873 George Brown, Jr., his brother, Andrew Brown, J.W. Bell and Albert Harris were jointly indicted for the murder of R.S. (Rat) Morrow in Montague County on September 5, 1873.

The officials presiding at that term of court were District Judge C.C. Brinkley, District Attorney F.E. Piner, District Clerk W.A. Morris, and Sheriff W.T. Waybourn.

In 1873 George Brown, Jr. was convicted in Denton County for the offense of aggravated assault. He assaulted a man "with a certain stick, of the length of three feet, and of the thickness of one inch, which said stick was then and there a deadly weapon." The name of the assaulted person, or the punishment given is not shown in the incomplete records of the trial. He was tried before County Judge Thomas E. Hogg.

Some time prior to George Brown, Jr.'s trial for the murder of R.S. Morrow he was tried for another murder. The time and place of the trial, the person murdered, or the results of the trial, are not known. However, there is mention of such other murder trial in the records of Brown's trial for the murder of Morrow.

George Brown, Jr. was tried for the murder of R.S. Morrow before a jury in Montague County on November 7, 1876. The officials presiding at that time were District Judge J.A. Carroll, County Attorney A.L. Matlock, District Clerk M.D. Herbert and Sheriff Lee N. Perkins.

R.S. Morrow resided in the same community on Farmer's Creek as the parties indicted for his murder. There had been previous trouble between Morrow and the Brown family. There was a public road on which George Brown, Sr. lived, and which, at the distance of about a mile, passed his son Jesse's, and, about a quarter of a mile further on, passed the residence of R.S. Morrow, who was commonly called Rat Morrow. Morrow's murder was accomplished by shooting him from ambush as he, his little son, and a companion were riding along the road.

The State's principal witness was Mrs. Lucinda Barras, a sister of George Brown, Jr. She was seventeen years old, and married, at the time of the trial, and about fourteen, and unmarried, when the murder was committed in 1873. She testified that early on the day of the killing she was at her father's house. Jesse Brown and his wife came over to her father's before the family had finished breakfast. Jesse told Andrew and George Brown, Jr., Alfred Harris and Stephen Sullivan to hurry and get through eating before Rat Morrow came along after his mules; and pretty soon the boys all started off with their guns toward the place where Morrow was later killed; that Jesse Brown and his wife wanted Lucinda to go over to their house and stay with their children, and Jesse told her to take a bucket of water along for the boys; that she started about a half hour after the boys had left, and took a bucket of water with her, and, when she got to where a branch crossed the road leading from her father's to Jesse's she found the boys there, lying in the branch, Sullivan and George, Jr. being on one side of the road, and Andrew and Harris on the other, each party having a gun and all having pistols; that from the talk that morning she knew they were going to kill Morrow – Jesse having said that if Morrow was not killed, the Browns could not live in that country; that she left the water with them, and went on over to Jesse's, and about three o'clock in the afternoon she saw Morrow, his little boy, and Mr. Koozier pass Jesse's place on horseback, going towards her father's; that they had been gone about long enough to go after Morrow's mules and return, when Koozier came back, running his horse at full speed, and went up to where Morrow lived, and directly Morrow's wife came down the road by Jesse's, cursing, and saying the Browns had killed her husband, and she would have them all killed before tomorrow night; at which Lucinda became frightened and returned to her father's, but by a route that did not pass the place where Morrow was killed; when she got home and told what Mrs. Morrow said, her father and Jesse got on their horses and started to Montague; that George, Jr. was not at the house when she got back there, and she did not see him for two or three days, when she was told to carry him something to eat, back of her father's house on a branch; and several days later she carried him something to eat in her brother Jesse's field; he did not come home to stay until Mrs. Morrow had been killed and Koozier had disappeared; neither Morrow or Koozier were armed on the day of the killing.

Lucinda denied on cross examination that she hated her brother, or had ever said that she would do what she could against him on account of his opposing her marriage to Sampson Barras. She was asked, but not allowed to answer, whether she was not a witness against George, Jr. in another murder case, in which her husband had turned state's evidence against him.

Sampson Barras, Lucinda's husband, testified for the State that about three months before the trial he and George, Jr. went from George Brown, Sr.'s to Jesse's place, and back again; that George showed him where

Morrow was killed, but told him he must not say anything about it. The place was close to a ravine which crossed the road. That George, Jr. said that he and the others were sitting in the ravine, and when Morrow passed along the road they all shot; that Morrow fell, and then one of them ran up and shot him under the chin.

On cross examination Barras said that he and George, Jr. had been on friendly terms; but that "of course I had some bad feelings towards him about the killing of Morrow, after he had told me, and ever since I have not had good feelings" towards him. Barras was asked, but not allowed to answer, whether there had not been some bad blood between he and George ever since he had turned State's evidence against George in another murder case.

Abe Wallace, for the State, testified that he was at home and heard four or five shots when Morrow was killed; that Mrs. Morrow sent him word about it, and he was the first person to get to the body. Morrow was lying on his back, dead. He had been shot in the elbows of both arms, in the back, under the chin, and in the right shoulder. The shot under the chin passed through the mouth, powder-burning the whiskers and tearing out the tongue. His hat was laying on the ground about seventy-five yards from the body, and at a spot where it appeared the horses had broke into a run, about half-way between Jesse's and George Brown, Sr.'s place. About eight o'clock the night before, Wallace met Albert Harris and George, Jr. in the road between Jesse's and George, Sr.'s. They said they had been to Montague for powder and shot, and that they were going to George Brown, Sr.'s. Wallace knew that there had been a difference between Morrow and the Browns, but he did not know any of the details.

John Southerland, for the State, testified that, some eighteen months before the trial, George Brown, Jr. showed him the place where Morrow was killed, saying there was where "one damned thief bit the earth." Southerland asked him who it was, and he said it was Rat Morrow. Southerland then asked him who did it, and he answered, "Me and Andy was two of the mavericks," and mentioned two others, whose names Southerland did not remember. At the time of this conversation, Southerland had known George, Jr. for about three months. Southerland did not tell any one what he had been told until all of the Browns were in jail. He was afraid they or some of their friends would kill him.

George Howard, witness for the State, was the second man to get to the body of Morrow. His testimony was in all essential details the same as that of

Abe Wallace.

Dr. J.A. Gordon, for the State, testified that he saw and examined the body of R.S. Morrow about an hour after he was killed; that he was killed by gunshot wounds, some of which were made with buck-shot; the shot under the chin was made with buck-shot, and the teeth and tongue were out on the whiskers; the shots in the face and in the back were mortal, and Dr. Gordon thought there was also a shot in the head; that the body was found in Montague County, and at the place where the killing occurred.

Mrs. Adaline Brown, for the defense, testified that she is the wife of Jesse Brown; that she and her husband were at George Brown, Sr.'s house the day that Morrow was killed; that she sent Lucinda Brown, now Barras, over to her house to stay with her children; she saw Lucinda when she started, and did not see her take a bucket of water with her.

She heard the guns when Morrow was killed; they were in a Southeast direction. Not more than two minutes before they were fired, George, Jr. and Stephen Sullivan started from the house, where they had been all day, to go over to Mr. Bell's to see their girls. They went in a Northeast direction, and had not got out of sight when the guns were fired. She saw them just before the firing, and just after it, and they had no guns. Andy Brown was close by the house when the guns were fired.

Mrs. Elizabeth Brown, wife of George Brown, Sr., and mother of George Brown, Jr., for the defense, testified that she heard the firing when Morrow was killed, and George, Jr. was at the house just before it commenced; he and Sullivan had both been sick, and were still puny, but had been talking about going over to old man Bell's. Andy was just coming to the house as the firing commenced; he had been sent to hunt a horse, and was returning, and was about 300 yards off. George, Jr. and Sullivan had left the house, but were not out of sight. She said that George, Jr. did leave the house later, and did not return home, but lay out to keep from being tried for the killing of Morrow; he did not come home until after Mrs. Morrow had been killed.

Nanny Hart, for the defense, testified that she heard Mrs. Lucinda Barras, since her marriage, say that she hated her brother, George, and would do all she could against him. Nanny said that she is a sister-in-law of Andy Brown.

Mrs. Addington, for the defense, testified that she had heard Lucinda

Barras say that she hated her brother George; that he had opposed her marriage to Sampson Barras, and should never have come about her when she moved out to herself. Mrs. Addington is the mother-in-law of Jesse Brown.

Mrs. Bettie Brown, wife of Andrew Brown, for the defense, testified that she heard Lucinda Barras say she would do anything against George that she could do, and that she wished he was dead and in hell; and, since the arrest of George, Jr., she heard Lucinda say, if Sampson Barras had sworn anything against George, Jr., Dave Price and George Howard made him do it.

J.H. Boggus and Dr. William Crump, for the defense, testified that they each knew the reputation of Sampson Barras, and that it was bad.

The jury found George Brown, Jr. guilty of First Degree Murder and assessed the death penalty. A.J. Hagler was Foreman of the jury. He appealed and the case was reversed and remanded for a new trial. If George Brown, Jr. was ever tried again for this murder, it does not appear on record. It is believed that he was never re-tried, because before this trial on November 7, 1876, he had already been arrested for the murder of Doc McClain in Montague County on May 1, 1876. He was tried for that murder, along with his brother Andrew Brown, on a change of venue to Denton County, in February 1878. The next chapter of this work deals with that trial and its result.

The indictment for the murder of R.S. Morrow against J.W. Bell was dismissed on March 16, 1875; against Andrew Brown, on March 21, 1876; and was also later dismissed against Albert Harris.

Stephen Sullivan was also indicted for the murder of R.S. Morrow, but it appears that he was never tried either.

Sampson Barras was later to be involved in the McClain murder.

Nothing further appears on record concerning the killing of Mrs. Morrow or the disappearance of Mr. Koozier. Both of these events occurred within a few days after the killing of R.S. Morrow.

George Brown, Jr. was represented by Attorneys Henry Hardy, W.S. Jameson and S.L. Shoemaker.

THE HANGING OF THE BROWN BROTHERS

On May 1, 1876, Doc McClain was shot and killed near a place called Chestnut Ford Crossing on Farmers Creek, in Montague County.

On October 30, 1876, the October Term of court began. Presiding were District Judge J.A. Carroll, County Attorney A.L. Matlock, District Clerk M.D. Herbert and Sheriff Lee N. Perkins.

The Grand Jury was composed of Wm. Broaddus, Foreman; John J. Willingham, B.F. Hodges, Jas. A. Strong, J.G. Hardy, Wm. Dixon, L.C. McNatt, P.S. Hagy, J.M. Grayson, R. Cook, J.C. Bryant, and J.P. Woodson.

On November 3, 1876, the Grand Jury indicted George Brown, Jr. and Andrew Brown for the murder of Doc McClain, and in the same indictment charged George Brown, Sr. and Jesse Brown as accomplices.

In another indictment, George Brown, Sr., Jesse Brown, Thomas White and George Ross were also indicted for murder.

On June 9, 1877, this indictment was transferred to Denton County on a change of venue.

In February 1878, the case against George Brown, Jr. and Andrew Brown, for murder, and against Jesse Brown, as an accomplice, went to trial before a jury in Denton County. The case against George Brown, Sr., as an accomplice, was severed and did not go to trial. The case was tried before J.A. Carroll, District Judge.

J.C. Stephens, for the State, testified that he was acquainted with George Brown, Sr., George Brown, Jr., Andrew Brown and Jesse Brown, and remembers that a man named Doc McClain was killed on Farmers Creek in May 1876, but did not know him personally. He was Justice of the Peace, Precinct No. 1, Montague County, and, as such, held an inquest on the body.

He first saw the body lying on the ground on Farmers Creek, at a point near Chestnut Ford Crossing. The breast appeared to have been penetrated by twelve or fourteen buckshot. There was also a wound in the side, lower down, and larger than those in the breast; and, in the opinion of Stephens, it was made by a pistol-ball.

About twenty steps West and North from where the body lay, there was a bank or ravine. The ravine appeared to have been washed out on the side, the wash making a kind of second bank, which was some two or three feet from the top of the first bank. Stephens could detect some dim tracks, which looked like some one had stood there. At the top some bushes were broken off. Stephens first saw the body on Sunday morning, where it appeared to have been lying for a couple of days. The body was buried near where it was found.

Stephens said that Mr. Sloss, Mr. Coffelt, Huse Robinson, Jesse Brown, George Brown, Jr., and others whom he does not remember, where present at the inquest. He does not think Andrew Brown was there. He remembers also that John Southerland was present.

Stephens heard Jesse Brown say that morning that he saw three strangers passing through the country the day McClain was killed, and that he suspected that they were the men who did the killing.

The body was lying about twenty steps from the ravine, and a person could stand on the second bank of the ravine and see it easily, where it was lying on the ground.

Mr. Jameson, one of the Defendant's Attorneys, got Stephens to go with him and take a view of the ground. Jameson held his hat up from the second bank, and Stephens saw his arm down to the elbow, from the road. He did not go into the ravine. He did not know of his own knowledge, but was told by Jr. Jameson, that he stood on the second bank of the ravine; the attorney may have been standing down in the ravine, and not on the second bank, though he told Stephens that he was standing on the second bank.

John Young Southerland, for the State, testified that he resided on Farmers Creek, where he had been residing for two years the past fall. He was not personally acquainted with McClain, but knows that he was killed in May 1876, by shooting. Southerland saw McClain just before he was killed; saw him killed, and saw him just after he was killed. He saw McClain walking along about one hundred yards, before he was shot. Southerland started out that morning to hunt a pony, and was on the road near Chestnut Ford Crossing, when he saw McClain coming across a small prairie, about two hundred yards off. He was going in the direction of a small ravine, near where he was killed.

In a few minutes after Southerland saw McClain, he saw George Brown, Jr., Andrew Brown, and Sampson Barras cross the road and go out of sight into the ravine. Southerland had dismounted to fasten his saddle, and was watching McClain, to ascertain who he was. McClain had walked about one hundred yards from where Southerland first saw him, and where he had reached a point about twenty steps from the ravine, when Southerland saw Andrew Brown, George Brown, Jr., Sampson Barras and John Barras rise up from behind the bank and shoot McClain. McClain fell, and George Brown, Jr. ran out, shot him with a pistol, and ran back into the ravine.

The three parties that Southerland saw ride up and go into the ravine all had shotguns. The four men who rose up and shot all had shotguns. Southerland did not see John Barras go into the ravine; does not know how he got there.

Andrew Brown was riding a dun pony, Sampson Barras a bay mule, and George Brown, Jr. a brown mule.

When the parties killed McClain, Southerland left the vicinity as fast as he could, going first to Mr. Adam's house and then to Mr. Glaze's, and from there home.

Southerland had a conversation with George Brown, Jr. a few days before the killing, in which Brown said that there was a bad set over at Johnson's, and that they were going over there "to get away with them." McClain lived at Johnson's. Southerland also had a conversation with Jesse Brown, at the schoolhouse, the day after the killing, in which Jesse asked, "Has George got you under good control?" Southerland responded that he didn't know; and Jesse then said that he wanted Southerland to go over there where the inquest was held, and tell those people that he, Southerland, saw three men from the Indian Nation, on the day of the killing, hunting for McClain, and that he expected they "got away" with him. Mr. Allen, a crippled schoolteacher, who boarded with Jesse Brown, was present at the conversation. Allen has fled the country.

Southerland did not tell of the killing, or what he knew about it, not even to his brother with whom he was staying, until after the Browns were arrested; and his reason for not doing so was, that he was afraid of the Browns and their friends. Southerland believed they would kill him, as he believed they had killed others for telling what they knew, and would not hesitate to kill him in the same way. He was afraid that his testimony alone would not convict the Browns.

Alvin Adams, for the State, testified that he lived near Eagle Point, but formerly lived near where the Browns live, and knows Andrew, George, and Jesse Brown, Sampson and John Barras. He and his brother, Blake, went to school to Ed Robertson on the day of the killing. On that morning he saw George and Andrew going in the direction of Chestnut Ford Crossing, and saw Sampson and John Barras with them at the time. Some of them were riding old man Brown's mules. He saw these men about eight o'clock A.M. When he first saw them they were crossing the road; did not stop at the branch. Alvin is now ten years old, and says that all of this transpired about two years ago. Ed Robertson boarded with Jesse Brown. He does not know whether the men were armed or not.

George Howard, for the State, testified that he lives on Farmers Creek; remembers when McClain was killed, and thinks the killing took place on Friday morning, some time in May, 1876. He was working for Jesse Brown on his farm, and had a conversation with him, just before the killing, about some of his, Howard's, horses that had been stolen. Jesse said that he expected that Johnson and McClain had stolen them, and that they would have to be killed. He had another conversation with Jesse, after the killing, in which Jesse said that he guessed a party from the Indian Nation had killed McClain; that he had sent word to them to come and get their thieves, and guessed they had got them.

Howard lived near Jesse Brown and on the morning of the killing, saw George Brown going around Jesse's field, towards home, between ten and twelve o'clock. He was riding Mr. Brown's brown mule, in a lope. Howard hallooed to him, but he did not stop, nor look towards him. His hat was pulled down over his eyes.

Joe Collier, for the State, testified that he knew McClain; he first knew him in Grayson County.

Collier had a conversation with Jesse Brown, after the killing, about a certain note he had received, warning him to leave the country. Collier asked Brown if he knew who sent it, or if he knew anything about it, to which Brown answered that he did not, and that if any body attempted to injure Collier, he would stand by him. – that they "hung up men like that." Collier then asked him if he knew who killed McClain; to which he replied that he supposed McClain was a thief, and that some one had followed him from the

Indian Nation, and "got away with him;" that he had sent them word to come and get their thieves, and he supposed they had done so. Collier then said to Brown, that if McClain was a thief, then his, Collier's, brother John was a thief, and asked why, if they killed McClain, they didn't kill John also; to which Brown answered, "Joe, you know you and I have been friends, and your brother John was a young man. I sent him word to get out of the country, to keep from being killed, as he was young, and there was a chance to reform him if he was a thief."

John Collier, for the State, testified that he knew the Browns; that he lived in Montague County when McClain was killed, and that he knew him well; that McClain was his partner. John Collier and McClain were living with Johnson when McClain was killed. John and McClain started out together early on that fatal Friday, to hunt their ponies, separating shortly and going different ways, since which time John has not seen McClain. John was uneasy about McClain, and fruitlessly hunted for him. On Saturday morning following the killing, John saw the Brown boys at work on an arbor at the schoolhouse. He told them that McClain was missing, and asked them to help hunt for him. John also told them that he was afraid something had happened to McClain, though he did not know that McClain had any enemies. To this Jesse Brown replied that McClain had more enemies than John knew of. Jesse and some of the other parties went with John towards the body. After separating from McClain on the morning of the killing, John heard some shooting, and took the party in that direction to where the body was found.

About ten o'clock on the morning of the killing, before John had got in from hunting the ponies, he was standing in a cow patch talking to a Mexican, who was trying to sell him a pistol, when George Brown rode up and asked John, "Where is Doc?" He was looking so pale and agitated that John asked him what was the matter, - if he was sick. George said that he was not sick then, but had just had a very severe attack of colic. George was riding his father's old brown mule. He then looked at the Mexican's pistol, and said, "Let me show you a pistol that is a pistol," – suiting his words by pulling out his pistol and showing it to the Mexican. The Mexican remarked that there was a load out of it; to which George responded that, as he was always shooting rabbits, he could not keep it always loaded. It was a large six-shooter, and chambered a 44 cartridge. The Mexican and others were with a cattle drove.

On Saturday, when Jesse Brown, John Barras, and others left the arbor to hunt for McClain, and after they had gone some distance, John Barras took

John Collier off to one side, gave him $2.00, and told him to leave the country, or he would be killed. John left accordingly, and did not see the body of McClain.

Joseph Sloss, for the State, testified that he was present at the inquest, and saw the body of McClain, which lay about twenty-two steps from a ravine on Farmers Creek. There was some paper found near the ravine, between the bank and the body, about five or six steps from the bank towards the body, that appeared to have been used as gun-wadding, and looked powder burnt. Sloss got down on the second bank, and could distinctly see the body where it lay. The bank was waist high. Sloss also stood in the road where Southerland stood, and could see and recognize a man standing on the second bank. Sloss later also went, in company with Mr. Coffett, John Southerland, Huse Robinson, Mr. Starkey, and others, and examined the grounds again.

J.C. Coffett, testifying for the State, says that he was present at the inquest. He examined the surrounding country, and saw the paper found near the bank of the ravine. He examined the washout, or second bank, and it was possible to see and recognize a man from the road, who was standing on the second bank. He distinctly saw and recognized Mr. Starkey and John Southerland, from the road while they were standing on the second bank.

William Adams, sworn for the State, deposed that he is the father of Alvin Adams, who was going to school when McClain was killed. He saw John Southerland on the morning of the killing. John stopped by his house; he had no business; was just visiting. John did not mention the killing of McClain to him.

Frank Willis, for the defense, testified that he is an attorney, residing in Montague, and that he knows and is familiar with the locality known as Chestnut Ford Crossing on Farmers Creek, and also the locality where McClain's grave is located. He stood on the second bank while Messrs. Hardy and Hamil tried the locality from several different points of view on the road, about two hundred and fifty yards distant. Willis, while on the second bank, could see the two men named, very plainly, on the road. If John Southerland was on the road, as he says he was, the Brown boys could have plainly have seen him from the ravine, had they been there. It is presumed that Frank Willis was trying to infer that no one would commit a murder in full view of a witness, and then let him escape to later identify them.

S.H. Hamil testified, for the defense, that he lives on Farmers Creek, near Chestnut Ford Crossing, and has at various times examined the locality where McClain was killed. Hamil has stood on the road, where Southerland says he was standing, and could not recognize a man standing on the second bank of the ravine. He could only tell that there was some one there. He could very plainly see a man standing on the top bank, and could tell it was a man, but could not recognize him. He knows John Southerland, and he stands about as well as any man in the community; knows nothing against his character.

Huse Robinson, for the defense, testified that he had examined the grounds in the vicinity of the grave, once with Mr. Jameson, one of the attorneys in the case, and J.C. Stephens, Esq. Robinson and Stephens stood on the road where Southerland said that he stood, and Mr. Jameson stood, as he said, on the second bank. Robinson could not see Mr. Jameson until he held up his hat; could then see the hat and a portion of his arm. Could see all of him when he stood on the top bank. He later examined the grounds in company with Sloss, Coffett, Starkey and others. That time he stood in the road and could recognize the parties standing on the second bank; could see them from the waist up. He does not know that Mr. Jameson, the Defendant's attorney, stood on the second bank; he said he did. He may have been standing at the bottom of the ravine. He did not go down in the ravine when he visited the vicinity with Mr. Jameson.

T.C. Pembroke next testified for the defense. He went with Mr. Hardy, one of the Defendant's attorneys, to take an observation of the grounds where McClain was killed. He took several views, from several different standpoints, on the road leading to Chestnut Ford Crossing. Mr. Hardy was down in the ravine. Pembroke discovered that from several different points on the road view was obstructed by timber and brush along the ravine. There was one place, some two hundred and fifty yards from the grave, where there is an unobstructed view. Mr. Hardy went down into the ravine, and said he stood on the second bank. He had his wife with him. Pembroke looked down there and could see no one until he held up his hat, which he could plainly see, together with a part of his arm. He does not know whether Mr. Hardy stood on the second bank or not. Pembroke did not go down into the ravine; he remained on the road at all times.

Mrs. Elizabeth Brown, for the defense, testified that she is the mother of George, Andrew and Jesse Brown, and is fifty-eight years old. She remembers the day that McClain was killed. George, Jr. lives at her home, and on that day was plowing in the field. She saw him in the field that morning about eight or nine o'clock. He went to work tolerably early; was not away before going to work, nor gone from the house or field before ten o'clock. He had no gun with him that day; if he had one, she would have seen it.

Andrew Brown came to the house early that morning, and was in the house until noon. He did not go away from the house for anything until noon. He was fixing his boots.

Sampson Barras is her son-in-law. George Brown, Sr. owns a black and sorrel mule, but did not own a yellow mare. Andrew owned a yellow mare, and rode her from his home to Mrs. Brown's home that morning. Martha Shockley, her granddaughter, rode the mare back to Andrew's home that morning. George, Jr. was plowing the black mare in the field all day on Friday, the day of the killing. George Brown, Sr. went over to Gus Johnson's that evening, about two hours of sun, to get his corn-drill.

Bettie Brown, wife of Andrew Brown, testified that her husband stayed at home all night the night before the killing. He was there the next morning, and went nowhere until he went over to his father's, which was about eight o'clock. He went straight to his father's house, because she followed him speedily to the parents' home. When she got there he was mending a bridle; he did not go away from the place all day. She saw George, Jr. working in the field through the day. Sampson Barras stayed at Andrew's house the night before the killing, and was riding Mr. Brown's sorrel mule. She saw Andrew's shotgun under the head of the bed after he left. She remembers that Rat Morrow was killed, but does not remember the day, month or year. She thinks that Andrew went to town the day after Morrow was killed. She does not know where he was when Morrow was killed, but he was at home when Freeman Batchelor was killed. She saw George Brown, Sr. working in a clearing all day. She is certain he stayed there all day.

Nannie Hart, testifying for the defense, says that she was at Andrew's house on Thursday night before the killing. Andrew was at home all that night, and was there next morning. She saw him when he started to go to his father's place, which was about eight or nine o'clock. Her mother started her, to catch up with Andrew, to get him to come back and sew up a wounded pony. She could see Andrew along the road all the way, but could not catch up with him. She saw him hitch his pony and go into the house. Mr. Brown was working in the clearing near the house. She saw George, Jr. plowing in the field with the old man's mule. Sampson Barras lived at Mr. Brown's house, but spent the night at Andrew's the night before the killing.

Josie Shockley, testifying for the defense, says that she is a near neighbor of the Browns, living one-half mile West of Mr. Brown's and one-half mile East of Andrew's. On the Friday morning she saw Andrew riding past her house, going towards his father's place, and remembers that he had no gun. It was about eight o'clock. Mrs. Shockley went down to Mr. Brown's a few minutes after he had passed, and found him there in the house. She stayed there until about noon, helping to churn; and when she left, Andrew was still there. George, Jr. was working in the field. Neither of the boys went away from the place that day. Mrs. Shockley's son is married to one of the Brown girls.

The jury found both George Brown, Jr. and Andrew Brown guilty of First Degree Murder, and sentenced both of them to be hanged. The jury acquitted Jesse Brown as an accomplice. Whether George Brown, Sr. was ever tried is not known. The burning of the courthouse in Denton in 1896 destroyed all prior records.

Sampson Barras was indicted for two different murders, in two separate indictments, during the June Term of 1878. The remaining records do not show for whose murders he was indicted. The burning of the courthouse in 1873 destroyed all prior records, and the burning of the next courthouse in 1884 destroyed all records not kept in vaults.

The June Term began on June 3, 1878. Presiding were District Judge J.A. Carroll, County Attorney A.L. Matlock, District Clerk M.D. Herbert, and Sheriff Lee N. Perkins.

The Grand Jury was composed of W.A. Morris, Foreman; W.R. Willingham, K.G. Heard, T.J. Williams, Jas. Davenport, John Orr, Jasper Field, Jas. Cheek, Wm. Dixon, Jas. C. McDaniel, Dean McDonald, C.F. Wilson, and Thos. Willis.

On June 11, 1878, Sampson Barras entered a plea of guilty to both indictments before a jury. He was found guilty of Second Degree Murder in the first case, and his punishment was assessed at 30 years in the penitentiary. He was found guilty of Second Degree Murder in the second case, and his punishment was assessed at 5 years in the penitentiary.

If John Barras was ever indicted for the murder of Doc McClain the records in that case are missing.

Both George Brown, Jr. and Andrew Brown appealed their death sentences, but both cases were affirmed by the Texas Court of Appeals in 1879.

The Brown brothers were represented by Attorneys W.S. Jameson and Henry Hardy of Montague. They were both excellent attorneys, and the Court of Appeals commented in its opinion to the effect that they had most ably represented the defendants during the trial.

George Brown, Jr. and Andrew Brown were both executed in the fall of 1879 in the City of Denton, Denton County. They were executed by the Sheriff of Denton County. They were executed in succession from a single gallows. George Brown, Jr., the younger of the two brothers, was executed first, followed within a few minutes by his brother Andrew. The gallows was erected on the South side of the courthouse, on the public square.

No member of the Brown family ever came to see the boys while they were held in the Denton County Jail. No one claimed their bodies after the execution. They were given a pauper's funeral by the county. They were buried in a section of the Denton City Cemetery that had been set aside for the county for use in pauper's funerals.

A sandstone marker, which was a kind commonly used in those days, was erected at their graves. The markers simply gave their respective names, and was followed by the word EXECUTED. Those markers are still standing.

Because of the burning of the Denton County courthouse in 1896, there are no records concerning this double execution. The above information has just been handed down by word of mouth.

A BANK ROBBER IS KILLED

About midnight on a cold, snowy winter night in November or December 1906, Pat Flannigan, a bank robber, was killed during an attempted burglary of the Citizens State Bank in Montague.

W.G. Bralley, a security guard, slept in the bank at nights. His room was located just to the rear of the vault. The vault was located about two-thirds of the way back from the front of the bank. The bank was located in the building now occupied by the Carminati Brothers as a grocery store, which is on the Southwest corner of the public square. The building faces North, running North and South. There was a hallway on both the East and West sides of the vault, leading from the bank room to the rear room in which Mr. Bralley slept.

Mr. Bralley was awakened by the noise of someone forcing open the rear door. Mr. Bralley hurried out of bed and slipped down the West hallway to the front of the vault. There he waited for the burglar to enter. He was standing against the West wall a few feet in front of the vault.

The burglar, which proved to be two burglars instead of one, came down towards the front of the vault using the East hallway. As the burglars came in sight from the hallway, Mr. Bralley opened fire. The front burglar returned the fire. The rear burglar turned and ran back down the East hallway towards the rear door. Mr. Bralley fired again and the burglar fell to the floor. The burglar had apparently got off only one shot, and missed. Mr. Bralley had got off two shots, and had not missed with either. The front burglar died there in the East hallway near the front of the vault. The hole made by the burglar's only shot is still visible in the West wall of Carminati's Grocery.

Mr. Bralley rushed past the fallen burglar in pursuit of the second burglar. However, by the time Mr. Bralley reached the rear door of the bank, the second burglar was rushing towards a buggy which he parked a distance down the alley so as not to attract attention by being parked around the bank. Mr. Bralley fired a couple of times at him but missed because of the distance.

Returning to the bank, Mr. Bralley found the first burglar dead. He then summoned help to get notice to the sheriff of the attempted burglary. Nearby neighbors, hearing the shots fired in the alley at the second burglar, began getting up to see what was going on. One of them was sent to notify the sheriff.

J.C. Bryant was sheriff at the time. He lived about one-half mile North of Montague, in the house later owned and occupied by John Carminati, and still occupied by his widow, Mrs. Delphena Carminati. His son, Cleve Bryant, was sleeping in the county jail at nights as a security guard. He was notified at the jail, and asked to notify his father. Sheriff Bryant arrived soon and took charge of the investigation.

R.B. Parker, a professional photographer from Gainesville, was in Montague, and was camping nearby in a covered wagon. He had been in Montague several days soliciting work. Sheriff Bryant summoned him to make photographs of the dead burglar, to be used for identification purposes.

Meantime, others had been sent in pursuit of the fleeing burglar. Their pursuit ended in Bowie early the next morning, when they located the buggy, but were never able to get any information as to the fleeing burglar. The horse and buggy proved to have been stolen from Dr. M.F. Sherrill in Montague. The horse was covered all over with white sweat foam, and had apparently been run hard all night. It almost died from the ordeal.

Through police photographs of known bank robbers and burglars, Sheriff Bryant was able to identify the slain bank burglar. His name was Pat Flannigan, the name Pat probably being short for the name Patrick, an Irishman from Kansas. He was a known safe picker, bank robber and burglar. His wife was notified of his death, and she came to claim the body. His body was shipped back to Kansas by train.

The second burglar was never located. It has often been told that Mr. Bralley said he thought he knew who the second man was, and thought him to be a local man. But because it was dark, in the bank hallway, and he only saw his back in the alley, and that only in the moonlight, and on a snowy night, he could not be sure. And since he could never be sure, and wanted to wrong no one, he would never say.

The following year, in 1908, Mr. Bralley ran for and was elected sheriff. He served from January 1, 1909, until he resigned on December 20, 1911, to move to Wichita Falls.

A.W. Cunningham, who was Mr. Bralley's chief deputy, was appointed sheriff on December 20, 1911, to succeed Sheriff Bralley. Mr. Cunningham served as sheriff through 1916, having been twice elected after his appointment.

No trial, of course, resulted from this incident, but the writer felt that it would, nevertheless, be an interesting item to present.

Pat Flannigan, who was killed in 1906 during attempted nighttime burglary of the Citizens State Bank in Montague.

THE KILLING OF WALKER HARGROVES

Bowie, in 1906, 1907 and 1908 was more of a hell-roaring western town than most of those in fiction. Saloons, frosty joints, gambling houses and pool halls were everywhere. A great many of them were located along Smythe Street. There had been so many shootings on Smythe that it became known as "Smokey Row." Saloon operators and gamblers were in control of the town.

One of the most unsavory characters on Smokey Row was Walker Hargroves. He had moved to Bowie from Arlington, where he had killed two men in a fight and shoot-out at the railroad station. He killed one of the Jarret boys after moving to Bowie. How many men he had killed, no one really knew. The number had been estimated to be seven or eight. He was the fastest man on the draw ever to be in these parts. He ruled Smokey Row with an iron hand, and he ruled out of fear. People were even afraid to mention his name in a conversation.

The good people of Bowie decided to clean the town up. The first thing to do was vote the saloons out. In 1906 a local option election was held. This was not the first election, but this was the first one to carry. The election was preceded by parades. Several hundred people, known as "pros," wearing white ribbons and singing, "The Fight is On" and "Onward Christian Soldiers," marched around the square, and even down Smokey Row. The "antis," wearing red ribbons, stood on the sidewalks and jeered the "pros."

The only trouble was, the saloon men wouldn't close up after prohibition was voted in. When arrested by local officers, they would simply make bond, or pay their fine, and keep operating. Law enforcement had broken down. The local City Marshall and the night watchman, which was all the police Bowie had, were just not able, try as they did, to cope with the situation. The Sheriff, with the time that he could spare them, was still not enough.

About 8:00 or 8:30 on the evening of March 28, 1907, shots once again rang out on Smokey Row. City Marshall John Wales and Night Watchman John Adams were sitting on a raised portion of the sidewalk in front of Giles Grocery. Giles Grocery was located on the corner of Wise and Smythe Streets. Walker Hargroves and his brother, Bob Hargroves, who had been imported for the occasion from Fort Worth, came down the street from Hargroves Saloon, passed within three or four feet of the officers, turned left on Wise Street, whirled and came back with their guns smoking. Wales was shot in the lung, and Adams received a glancing shot across the forehead, which caused blood to fall down over his face. Both officers drew their guns, but Wales' gun was shot from his hand. Adams was firing wildly and shot a man across the street. The man was hit in the stomach and later died. The Hargroves brothers lit out for Walker's home, where they holed up.

It appeared that John Wales was going to die. Mr. Wales thought, too, that he was going to die. So, later that night, he made his sons, Roy and Curt, swear to him that they would kill the Hargroves.

Things began to happen fast. The local hardware store was opened up, guns, pistols and ammunition was passed out. A mob was formed. The mob went to Hargroves' home, surrounded it and demanded Hargroves to surrender. They threatened to dynamite the house, or set fire to it. Hargroves called out that his wife and child were in the house. This sobered the mob up somewhat.

In the meantime, Sheriff B.F. Watson had started from Montague, a distance of twelve miles away, on horseback. Upon arriving at Hargroves' house, he hollered out, "Walker, I'm coming in after you." "I'll kill you if you set foot in this house," Hargroves responded. "All right," the Sheriff said, "if you kill me, I'm in my shirt sleeves, because I'm coming in unarmed." As he went in, he somehow or other managed to persuade Hargroves to surrender. The Sheriff slipped Hargroves out of the house in the darkness, took him to jail at Montague, where Hargroves made bond and left for Wichita Falls.

The next day not a saloon opened in the outraged town. A meeting was called that night in the opera house by a banker, Sterling P. Strong. Several hundred persons attended. A resolution was passed ordering the saloon men to get their whiskey and beer out of Bowie within thirty days; otherwise, the citizens would take charge of it.

The resolution was dated March 29, 1907, and was executed by five Bowie citizens for the group, and by Jas. A. Graham, an attorney representing the liquor interest, and the resolution read as follows:

THE STATE OF TEXAS   )
COUNTY OF MONTAGUE   )

KNOW ALL MEN BY THESE PRESENTS:

That we, the undersigned citizens of Bowie fully realizing the gravity of the situation of affairs in Bowie and knowing well and being determined that all manner of joints and places containing intoxicating liquors in Bowie will and shall be immediately and permanently closed; hereby recommend that the contents of each of said joints be delivered to a committee selected by the citizens of Bowie for purpose of storage in a single building to be under the complete supervision of said committee for 30 days and that same will not be molested or destroyed if acts of good faith on the part of said proprietors are evidenced to fully carry out this agreement and that they are evidenced to fully carry out this agreement and that they will procure places and remove same from said place of storage and from Montague County within 30 days and if they fail or refuse to do this then our further obligation in all matters cease. And the delivery of said committee by said proprietors shall be an acceptance of the conditions hereof.

March. 29, 1907

John Speer
Sneed Strong
C.H. Boedeker
A.E. Thomas
Sam Young
Jas. A. Graham

  With both of their city officers wounded, the citizens of Bowie Appealed to the Governor for help. The Governor sent two Texas Rangers, Thomas B. White and Oscar Rountree, up from Austin. They were very impressive in their large white hats, their pearl-handled pistols and cowboy boots. They moved in and immediately began closing all saloons, frosty joints and pool halls. They arrested all of owners, operators and employees. They also arrested all known gamblers. Bowie had only one small one-room calaboose, so the Rangers chained their prisoners out in the open. As soon as the prisoners could be processed, may of them paid their fines and began leaving Bowie. The Rangers closed the town of Bowie down tight.
  Meantime Hargroves had let it be known that he wasn't going to take his liquor out of town. He said that he would kill anyone who messed with it. So, at the end of the 30-day period, a mob formed under the leadership of

Sterling P. Strong, smashed open the doors of the saloons, loaded the whiskey and other intoxicants on horse drawn floats, and carried them to the railroad station to ship them to Fort Worth. But Hargroves had put the railroad on notice not to accept the shipment, so they refused.

The mob proceeded down across the railroad tracks to a point on the branch between the wagon yard and the old third ward school, unloaded the whiskey, crates, cases and barrels, smashed them with axes and set fire to it.

After his saloon had been looted, and his whiskey burned, Walker Hargroves left for Fort Worth. But soon word was whispered around that Hargroves was coming back; that he had five men on his list to kill. They were John Wales, who was slowly recovering; the two Texas Rangers; Sterling P. Strong, and a barber named Porter Brodie.

One day soon thereafter, just before noon, a man rode through town on horseback shouting, "Hargroves is in town! Hargroves is in town!" Everyone knew what this meant. Mr. Wales knew, the Rangers knew, Porter Brodie knew, and so did everyone else.

In a few minutes guns were blazing once again on old Smokey Row. Just above Giles Grocery, about where Hargroves Saloon was, two men were shooting it out in the street. Everyone just knew that it was John Wales and Walker Hargroves. However, it was not John Wales. He had gone to the bank with the two Rangers to get a rifle when the shooting began.

Hargroves, in keeping with the badman custom of the times, got lordly drunk and walked down past the humble little barber shop of Porter Brodie, which was near his saloon. Porter was a quiet, inoffensive man, but on the side of law and order. He had expressed himself openly on the liquor question. So, his name was on Hargroves' list. When Porter Brodie saw Hargroves pass, he picked up his 45, walked out on the sidewalk, fired into the ground to let Hargroves know the fight was on, and they squared off and began shooting.

Porter would lay his 45 across his left elbow for a rest, fire, then step out of the smoke and go through the same procedure again.

Hargroves must have been really drunk, or else he would have killed Brodie out of his superior experience. He was known to be one of the fastest guns ever to come to this area. Or it may be that, like many bullies he got excited when braced by an unexpected and valiant adversary.

When Brodie had emptied his gun, he ran over and began to club Hargroves on the head with the butt-end. Then one of Hargroves' henchmen, a man named Craig, ran up behind Brodie and struck him down with something, while other sympathizers pulled Hargroves into Smith's meat market.

Brodie staggered down the street and across the railroad tracks. He was telling those that he passed enroute that, "Boys, I don't know whether I killed him or not, but I done the best I could." Brodie was bleeding from a glancing wound on his temple, and a shot in his foot. There wasn't a hospital in Bowie, but Brodie refused to even go to the doctor's office. He walked five or six blocks to his home.

It later developed that Brodie had hit Hargroves with every shot. That only the breastplate Hargroves was wearing saved him from death.

Since there was no hospital in Bowie, Hargroves had to be sent to Fort Worth where his wounds could be treated and attended to. He was placed on a cot and carried to the railroad station. He was pale, his eyes were closed, and he lay there near death. When the 2:08 train to Fort Worth pulled in, he was lifted into the baggage car. Some doctor had bandaged him up for the trip. He did survive his wounds, as did John Wales, John Adams and Porter Brodie.

In May, 1908, the people of Bowie learned that Walker Hargroves had been killed in Fort Worth. He was killed in a saloon by a bartender named Walter James. Hargroves was drunk and began breaking glasses in the saloon. James ordered him to stop. Hargroves made a move as if to draw. The bartender whipped a shotgun out from under the counter and according to the report, "blew his brains out." There were no eyewitnesses to the shooting. John White, a Negro porter in the saloon heard the trouble start, but he went to the rear of the saloon. A few minutes later he heard the shot, and when he returned to the front Hargroves was stretched out on the floor apparently dead.

City Detective Ben U. Bell said that he jumped off of a streetcar when he saw a bunch of people gathered in front of the Board of Trade Saloon. When he went in he saw Hargroves lying on the floor dead. Walter James said, "Well, I guess you had better take charge of me."

John White stated that Hargroves came into the saloon about 4:00 o'clock P.M. White said Hargroves drank two beers, then ordered a third, and insisted that James, the bartender, drink it with him. James refused to do so. Hargroves insisted, using curse words and applying epithets to James. James finally consented to split the bottle with Hargroves. Hargroves broke a glass and said that he did it on purpose, still using curses. He backed from the bar with his hand on his pistol. James told him to quit calling him those names. After this, White went to the rear of the saloon.

Dr. M.V. Creagan hurried to the saloon immediately after the shooting. Hargroves was not quite dead, but breathed five or six times before expiring. He described Hargroves' wounds.

An article appearing in a Fort Worth paper under date of May 21, 1908 stated that Justice Maben had that day completed the inquest concerning the death of Walker Hargroves. The article stated that his funeral would be that afternoon. His funeral would be held from the family residence at 408 Missouri Avenue, at 2:00 o'clock, Friday. Rev. Waites of the Christian Tabernacle conducted the services. Internment was in Oakwood Cemetery.

An article appearing in the *Fort Worth Press* in November 1952, stated that Walter James, who had killed Walker Hargroves 44 years ago, in 1908, had died in Fort Worth at the age of 78 years.

In the Friday, May 22, 1908 issue of *The Saint Jo Tribune*, the following article appeared:

Walker Hargroves, formerly of Bowie and well-known character throughout this section was shot and instantly killed in the Board of Trade Saloon in Fort Worth at 5:15 Wednesday afternoon. Walter James, a bartender in the saloon, surrendered to the officers and was placed under a $5,000 bond, charged with the killing. According to reports, Hargroves got into a dispute with James and had started around the east end of the bar with the announced intention of "settling matters" when the fatal shots were fired that ended his checkered career.

On October 30, 1908, Porter Brodie was killed in Bowie by a man named Walter Smith, who was commonly known as Pat Smith. But that is another report in this work, which is entitled "The Killing of Porter Brodie."

THE KILLING OF PORTER BRODIE

Porter Brodie was a well-known Bowie barber during the stormy days on Smokey Row. He operated a modest little barbershop on Smythe Street, just a couple of doors from where Walker Hargroves had operated his saloon. He was a quiet, inoffensive man. However, he had very strong convictions against liquor. He had been quite outspoken on the subject. He had helped promote the local option election of 1906, which carried and brought prohibition to Bowie for the first time. There had been bad blood between Brodie and the saloon owners for some time, as evidenced by his shoot-out with Walker Hargroves on Smokey Row on an occasion in about May, 1907.

Walter Smith, who was commonly called Pat Smith, operated a frosty joint and pool hall on Smokey Row. At one time following the coming of prohibition to Bowie, Brodie had filed a complaint against Pat Smith for violation of the prohibition laws. The two Texas Rangers who were stationed in Bowie promptly arrested Smith. This had caused bad blood between Pat Smith and Porter Brodie.

About 2:00 o'clock P.M. on October 30, 1908, Brodie was returning to his shop from lunch. Just as he stepped upon the sidewalk, Pat Smith came walking up from the direction of Johnson's confectionery. Neither man spoke to the other. When they were about 18 or 20 feet apart, once again the guns were blazing on old Smokey Row. The shooting occurred in front of Giles Grocery on Smythe.

Either three or four shots were fired. Two bullets struck Bodie in the breast, in the region of the heart. A third bullet missed his body and cut a hole through the brim of his hat. Brodie was dead in about five minutes.

The only utterance of any kind came from Brodie. When the first shot struck him, Brodie said, "Oh." His body pitched forward. Before it reached the sidewalk, a second shot struck him and he said, "Oh, Lordy."

The body of Brodie lay on the sidewalk for an hour or more, surrounded by a large crowd, eager to get a look at it. The dead man, who was in his shirtsleeves, lay stretched out in the center of the sidewalk on his back, with his head towards the South. The left hand lay by his side. The right elbow rested on the sidewalk, with the hand on the breast. There was no gun on or near Brodie's body.

As soon as he could do so, Justice J.T. Stallings had the body removed to Burgess Funeral Home. Here Dr. J.T. Lawson, in the presence of Justice Stallings, stripped the body and examined the two wounds. Both bullets tended downward and backward after entering the body. It was the opinion of Dr. Lawson that both bullets passed through the heart, and that either would have caused death. The Justice and Doctor found no weapons on the body. After the official examination of the body, it was conveyed to the home of the deceased on the South side of town.

The community was profoundly shocked when the news of the tragedy spread over town.

Justice Stallings, sitting as Coroner, concluded his written verdict as follows: "That on the 30th day of October 1908, one Walter Smith, commonly known as Pat Smith, of his malice aforethought, in said County and State, did shoot the said deceased with a pistol, inflicting upon the breast and body of the deceased two gunshot wounds each of which penetrated the region of the heart from the effects of which said wounds the said deceased died at the time and place here before stated."

Shortly after the shooting, Pat Smith was taken into custody by Constable John Wales, charged with the shooting. When arrested Smith handed the officer a 45 pistol. Later in the day he was conveyed to the jail in Montague by Sheriff B.F. Watson.

On the following Friday afternoon and Saturday morning, after the shooting, Justice Stallings, sitting as Coroner, conducted an inquest on the shooting of Brodie. Assistant County Attorney J.N. Campbell, acting for County Attorney Charles F. Spencer, represented the State. The following testimony was produced during the inquest:

M.M. Huskey, farmer, seven miles South, was standing on Wise Street on crossing between Wilson's restaurant and Stoner's grocery store, 50 or 60 feet from Giles corner; heard a shot; looked up and saw a man falling on the sidewalk in front of Giles' store; as he fell a second shot was fired; when he fell the man who did the shooting stepped about one step towards the body and fired again; the last shot was after the man had fallen; saw no weapon of any kind in the hands of the man who was shot down; saw a pistol in the hand of the man who did the shooting; did not know the parties at the time; saw the man who did the shooting go up the street after he fired the last shot; he went into the Bowie Meat Market; he knew both men, Smith and Brodie, but did not recognize either of them at the time of the shooting; was among the first to get to the body of Brodie; he was lying on his back on the pavement with one hand by his side, the other with elbow on pavement and hang against his breast; he never moved, but could see that he was still alive; he gasped five or six minutes, and one time threw up his hand toward his face; didn't think he lived over 10 minutes after the shooting; three shots were all he heard; the first two were in quick succession; the last was fired as the body lay on its back on the pavement; the man fell with his head towards the man who did the shooting.

J.W. Davis, farmer, six miles North, was standing on the sidewalk, 20 feet below the Bowie Meat Market on Smythe Street, talking to Pat Smith about a little trade they had on hand the past Saturday; had up a forfeit; Smith went on down the street; he remained where he was, and was talking to W.F. Gunter until the shooting occurred, which was immediately afterward; he saw the shooting and saw Brodie fall; he fell on the street towards Davis; there were four shots fired; one shot just did miss him; at the second shot Brodie fell; two more shots were fired in qui k succession; three of the shots were fired in the opposite direction from him; saw the first shot fired; cannot positively swear who fired it; he knows the bullet passed him; he heard it; he was about 100 feet from where the shooting occurred and in plain view; the street was cleared when the first shot was fired.

W.M. McCarter was standing with M.M. Huskey when the shooting occurred. His testimony was substantially the same as Mr. Huskey's with this addition: he was one of the first to get to Brodie; he found him lying on his back, his left hand by his side; his right on his breast; Brodie was in his shirt sleeves; he had no weapon on or about him that he could see and there was none laying by him; he didn't think any one could have removed a pistol from his person or from the pavement near him without witness seeing it done.

T.C. McCracken was standing on the sidewalk on Smythe Street between Johnson's place and the place where Ezra Williams' pool hall is located; he was talking with Geo. Williams; his face was up the street and his back down; he heard a shot and turned around and looked; the first thing he saw was a man falling in front of Giles' store about 75 feet from him; two more shots were fired; he saw the man who fired the last two shots; he did not know at the time who he was, but as soon as he turned around and faced him he saw that it was Pat Smith; the man falling towards him when the second shot was fired, and was down on his back as well as he could see from where he was when the last shot was fired; he went at once to the man who was down and recognized him to be Porter Brodie; he was about the third man, maybe the fourth to reach him; he was in his shirt sleeves, lying on his back, one hand by his side and the other on his breast or near it; he saw no weapons or pistol, on or about Brodie; he did not think it possible for anyone to have removed a pistol from the body or the sidewalk near where he fell without witness having seen it done; he and old man Glover and Ed Sinclair placed his hat under his head just as he got there; he gasped a few times and died; in 10 or 15 minutes after he was shot he was dead; he was positive that only three shots were fired; as Pat Smith passed him after the shooting occurred he had a pistol in his hand and seemed to be trying to put it in his pocket or clothes; after the first shot there was a short interval then two more in quick succession; just as quickly as they could be fired he thought; he never heard a bullet whistle from either shot that was fired; he did not leave the sidewalk when the firing began and went to where Brodie lay as soon as the last shot was fired.

J.H. Cable, clerk at Giles' store, was standing just inside of Giles' store; he was about two feet, he supposed, from the North front door, which opens out on the pavement on the East side of Smythe; one door opens out on the corner of the building, and the one he was nearest to opens out on Smythe; there is still another front door that opens out on Wise Street, in front of the building; all three doors were standing open; he saw Brodie first; he had just stepped up on the edge of the sidewalk when he first saw him; he was going North, and towards his shop, two doors North of the Giles building; he was in his shirt sleeves; about the same time Brodie stepped up on the sidewalk he heard someone coming down the street and looked around and saw Pat Smith; he was walking pretty fast; about the time he observed him he stopped directly in front of the door where he was standing; he saw him reach down into his pocket as though he was pulling out a handkerchief, and pulled out a gun; he immediately raised it up and fired. Brodie, at the time Smith fired, was some 18 or 20 feet from him, walking toward him; he pitched forward when the first shot was fired; Smith fired again before Brodie hit the pavement; he fell on his shoulder and rolled over on his back; Smith took one step forward and fired another shot; Brodie was lying on his back when the last shot was fired; there was not a word said by either Smith or Brodie before the shooting began; he never heard a word said by either, except Brodie said, "Oh" and "Oh, Lordy;" he said "Oh" when the first shot was fired, and about the time he hit the sidewalk he said "Oh, Lordy;" witness saw no pistol or weapon of any kind in the hands of Brodie or about his person; he saw no pistol or weapon of any kind fall on the sidewalk when

Brodie fell; Smith went up the street and out of his sight immediately after firing the last shot; three shots, and only three shots, were fired, and Pat Smith fired all of them.

S.P. Johnson testified substantially the same as did Cable and Huskey, except that he said when Smith returned up the street he was carrying a pistol in each hand.

Smith's trial began on February 6, 1911. Judge Clem B. Potter presided. County Attorney Charles F. Spencer prosecuted the case.

It seems that Smith's defense should have been that there were four shots fired; that Brodie fired at him first but missed; that he then fired three at Brodie but didn't miss; that he then went over and picked up Brodie's gun and went up the street. See the testimony of Davis and Johnson. However, the list of defendant's witnesses does not give the name of either Davis or Johnson.

In any event, the jury returned a verdict of not guilty. The verdict was signed by J.R. Allgood, Foreman.

Walter (Pat) Smith was later to be shot on December 23, 1912 by Constable Harbin H. Edwards, from which wounds he died some four or five days later. See "The Killing of Walter (Pat Smith."

THE KILLING OF WALTER (PAT) SMITH

On December 23, 1912, the day before Christmas Eve, County Attorney Paul Donald and wife, Clara, were visiting with his parents when he received a call from John Adams, City Marshall. Marshall Adams told Mr. Donald that they were having a disturbance down on Smokey Row. This report must have come as no surprise to Mr. Donald, since fights, disturbances, shootings and killings seemed to occur all too often on old Smokey. This was true all during the rough and rowdy gun-toting days following the turn of the century.

Mr. Donald was requested by Marshall Adams to meet him in front of Brown's Drug Store, which was located where the Triple D is now located. Mr. Donald met the Marshall at the appointed place. The Marshall had also arranged for Constable Harbin E. Edwards and Deputy Sheriff John Wales to meet them.

Walter (Pat) Smith, who had formerly operated a frosty joint and pool hall on Smokey, but had been forced to close them with the coming of prohibition to Bowie, was now operating a grocery store in his old location. The disturbance was going on in Pat's grocery store. Marshall Adams and Deputy Wales stationed themselves in front of Pat's store. Smith's grocery was located next door to where the Fit Shop was located in recent years, which is about the middle of the block.

County Attorney Donald and Constable Edwards went around to the rear of the grocery store. As Mr. Donald and the Constable arrived at the rear door, a man named Pruener emerged. Mr. Pruener had been beaten to a pulp; so severely beaten that he was nearly beyond recognition. Pruener was taken by some men in the store to old Dr. Yakely's office, which was located upstairs over the old Chapman Building.

Pat Smith came out of the back door and encountered Donald and Edwards. Smith was clad in an overcoat and had his right hand in his pocket. Smith seemed to be fumbling or holding something in his coat pocket. The way Smith kept his hand in his coat pocket led both Donald and Edwards to believe that he had a gun in his pocket.

Smith looked at Paul Donald and said, "The alley is open at both ends, and you can leave at either end." To which Mr. Donald then replied, "I'm not about to leave." Smith then appeared about to draw the object from his coat pocket when Constable Edwards put his hand on Smith's shoulder and said, "Pat, don't do that." Smith then took his left hand and shoved Harbin Edwards in the face.

At this point Edwards drew his gun and fired three or four shots in rapid succession at Smith's midsection. Smith then turned and quickly staggered into the store. Donald and Edwards followed the wounded man. Inside the store they found a gun that Smith had supposedly placed on a barrel as he went through the store. Edwards picked up the gun and he and Donald continued to pursue the wounded man. Smith had gone out the front of the store and had progressed as far as Brown's Drug Store where he collapsed in front of it.

Pat Smith was carried home, where he lingered near death for four or five days before he finally died.

Other men were arrested in a nearby saloon by the peace officers for their part in the beating of Pruener.

Some time later Mr. Edwards was indicted and tried for the murder of Pat Smith. Paul Donald was the only living witness who could testify in Edwards' behalf. It may have been decided later that a trial should be had, while Mr. Donald's testimony was available, just as a protection to Mr. Edwards.

In any event, H.H. Edwards was indicted on January 16, 1915, in Cause No. 5843, in the District Court of Montague County. The Foreman of the Grand Jury was W.A. Philpot.

Apparently, on February 3rd, Mr. Edwards was tried. He pled self-defense. Paul Donald was his principal witness. He described the events that occurred immediately prior to the shooting. Edwards was acquitted.

The case was tried before Judge Charles F. Spencer. Paul Donald was the County Attorney; N.F. McClellan was District Clerk; and A.W. Cunningham was Sheriff.

Thus ends the saga of three men, Walker Hargroves, Porter Brodie and Pat Smith, who knew old Smokey Row. They knew its violence; they were a part of its violence; two of them died of its violence; the other almost died of its violence, and did die of violence in Fort Worth soon after leaving Smokey Row.

Most of the material for the last three chapters, dealing with the killings on Smokey Row, was taken from a series of articles written by former Governor James V. Allred, and later published by his brother, Renne Allred, Jr., in The Bowie News. Much of the wording of the last three chapters are in the Governor's own words.

CONCLUSION

Thus was the violence with which our forefathers lived; thus was the courage they possessed to suppress such violence; and thus were the sacrifices they made to secure for themselves, their children, and their children's children, a better life. We owe them so much more than we will ever know.

M.F. L.

0810317

STATE OF TEXAS §
COUNTY OF MONTAGUE §

VOL. 465 Page 291

ASSIGNMENT

KNOWN ALL MEN BY THESE PRESENTS that the undersigned William "Bill" London ("Assignor"), individually and as sole heir of Mary Lou London, deceased, and located at 222 West 4th Street., Loft #210, Fort Worth, Texas, FOR GOOD AND VALUABLE CONSIDERATION, receipt of which is hereby acknowledged, hereby irrevocably TRANSFERS, SELLS and ASSIGNS to the Montague County Historical Commission ("Assignee"), located at P.O. Box 161 Montague, Texas, as established under the laws and authority of the State of Texas and the Commissioner's Court of Montague County, Texas pursuant to Texas Local Government Code § 38.002, its successors and assigns, in perpetuity, all rights (whether now known or hereinafter invented), title, and interest, throughout the world, including any copyrights and renewals or extensions thereto, in:

- "County Officials of Montague County"
  - By Marvin F. London
- "Famous Court Trials of Montague County"
  - By Marvin F. London; United States : s.n., 1974
  - Saint Jo, Tex. : S.J.T. Printers
  - 345.76402 L847F
- "Indian Raids in Montague County"
  - By Marvin F. London; United States : s.n., 1977
  - Saint Jo, Tex. : S.J.T. Printers
  - 976.4541 L847I

IN WITNESS THEREOF, Assignor has duly executed this Agreement.

By: _____ Date: 11/19/08
William "Bill" London

STATE OF TEXAS §
COUNTY OF MONTAGUE §

Before me on November 19, 2008 personally appeared William "Bill" London, to me known to be the person who is described in and who executed the foregoing assignment instrument and acknowledged to me that he executed the same of his own free will for the purpose therein expressed.

_____
Notary Public

GEORGIA L. GRIFFIN
MY COMMISSION EXPIRES
July 5, 2010

FILED FOR RECORD: 12-1-2008 AT 10:16 A.M./P.M.
RECORDED: 12-1-2008 AT 5:00 P.M.
GLENDA HENSON, COUNTY CLERK, MONTAGUE COUNTY, TX

Made in the USA
Coppell, TX
11 March 2025

46960753R00063